Hearts in Transition
Navigating Love & Loss in Foster Care

Danielle Murphy

First published in Australia in 2025 by Murphy Publishing & Media

Copyright © 2025 by Danielle Murphy

All rights reserved.

ISBN: 978-1-7642728-1-3

No part of this book may be reproduced in any form or by any electronic or mechanical means, including information storage and retrieval systems, without written permission from the author, except for the use of brief quotations in a book review.

This book is a personal account of the author's experiences as a foster carer within the Australian out-of-home care system. It reflects her own perspectives, emotions, and interpretations of events as they occurred throughout my journey.

To protect the privacy and confidentiality of the children, families, agencies, and individuals involved, identifying details—including names, locations, timelines, and certain circumstances—have been changed or omitted. Any resemblance to actual persons, living or deceased, events, or organisations is purely coincidental unless explicitly stated.

The views and opinions expressed in this book are solely the author's and do not necessarily reflect those of any agency, organisation, or governmental body. This book is not intended to offer legal, medical, psychological, or professional advice. Readers seeking such advice should consult qualified professionals.

While every effort has been made to convey the experiences of the foster care journey accurately, memory is subjective, and interpretations may differ. This work is offered in the hope of shedding light on the realities, challenges, and profound rewards of foster care, with deep respect for all those who walk this complex path.

Praise for Hearts in Transition

Fostering is not merely about having a big heart and an empty room; it's a profound commitment that demands resilience, empathy, and unwavering dedication. Dani's narrative serves as a poignant reminder of the untold sacrifices and joys that come with embracing the role of a foster carer.

— Louise Allen, *Author, foster carer, charity founder, care experienced, public speaker*

This book speaks the truth of foster care with honesty, humility, and deep respect. As a proud Aboriginal woman from the Ngoorabul tribe, a grandmother, and a foster carer of 13 years, I've seen the beauty and the heartbreak that comes with caring for our kids. This story honours that journey. It is thoughtful, culturally respectful, and brave in the way it shares the hard parts, not shying away from the challenges but always holding the child at the centre. I felt seen in these pages. For anyone walking this path—carer, worker, or community member—this book is a must-read.

— Lanette Duck, *Proud Ngoorabul woman, mother, foster carer, and grandmother*

This important book will move you to tears and open your heart. A devastatingly honest portrayal of Australia's foster care system, it captures the heartbreak and joy of an Australian couple navigating a complex and bureaucratic world. I encourage everyone who has ever considered fostering—or who works within the child protection system—to read this powerful story of resilience, compassion, and hope.

— JASMIN NOLAN, *MOTHER, AGENCY WORKER, FOSTER CARER SUPPORT PERSON*

To my dearest husband. Your unwavering love and loyalty have been my anchor through it all. Thank you for standing by my side every step of the way.

To the children who have forever changed my life—you are not forgotten. Whether you stayed for years or just a moment, you hold a special place in my heart and always will.

To the family and friends who embraced our foster children with love and supported us through the hardest days—your kindness, encouragement, and generosity made all the difference.

Contents

Foreword	ix
Introduction	xi
1. Infertility	1
2. Yes, I Want to Adopt!	10
3. The Breaking Point	22
4. Embracing Temporary	42
5. Becoming Parents	56
6. Uncertainty & Working in the System	70
7. Placement Breakdown & Sibling Relationships	82
8. The Weight of Waiting	96
9. Reflections	106
10. A Better Way Forward	116
Appendix	125

Foreword
By Louise Allen

Fostering is a journey driven by compassion and personal experiences. The decision to open our homes stems from deep-rooted emotions and desires, often unrecognised until a moment of realisation. Dani's story mirrors the intricate reality of fostering, where the challenges far outweigh the initial expectations. It takes nerves of steel and the heart of a lioness to navigate the complexities of the system surrounding these children.

Dani's candid account sheds light on the emotional rollercoaster foster carers endure. The expectation to treat these children as our own, only to be reminded of their state-owned status, can be emotionally taxing. The fatigue we experience is not a lack of compassion but rather a result of the relentless demands of the system. Every foster carer resonates with the endless cycle of emails, reports, and meetings that often overshadow the primary focus – the children.

Adoption and fostering intertwine in profound ways, sharing the weight of emotional investment in the child's well-being. The blurred lines between personal and professional involvement can be overwhelming, especially when conflicting interests arise. Dani's narrative unravels the unspoken truths of fostering, offering a rare glimpse into the challenges faced behind the scenes.

Training for foster care often lacks the first-hand perspective of experienced carers. Dani's book stands out as an educational beacon, bridging the gap between theoretical training and practical realities. By sharing her unfiltered experiences, Dani provides a valuable insight that fosters a deeper understanding of the intricacies involved in nurturing vulnerable children.

Fostering is not merely about having a big heart and an empty room; it's a profound commitment that demands resilience, empathy, and unwavering dedication. Dani's narrative serves as a poignant reminder of the untold sacrifices and joys that come with embracing the role of a foster carer.

Louise Allen
Author, foster carer, charity founder, care experienced, public speaker
Louise-allem.com

Introduction

I write this book as I prepare to say goodbye to two children who have wrapped themselves around my heart. The thought of letting them go is soul-crushing. This isn't the first time I've faced such heartbreak, and it won't be the last. Saying goodbye to foster children is a unique and emotional journey, one filled with heartache, hope, and transformation. Through sharing my experiences, I hope to provide comfort and understanding to those who may find themselves in similar situations.

This book is not just about me or my story. I share it because the challenges we've faced are not unique—many carers, children and families walk similar roads. Too often, those struggles happen in isolation, leaving people feeling unheard and invalidated, which can be the hardest part of all. Our journey through infertility, attempted adoption, and foster care is simply a window into a much bigger reality. My hope is that by telling our story, I can raise even a little more awareness of the realities that foster carers, adoptive parents, and children live with every day.

I want to be clear from the outset that while this book shares deeply personal experiences—including my longing to be a mother—my highest priority has always been the well-being, safety, and stability of the children in my care. I believe in child-centred practice and permanency planning that serves the best interest of each child, even when that means advocating for their transition to family members instead of staying with me. Loving these children means wanting what is best for them—even when that comes at a personal cost.

A little about me—I'm Canadian by birth, but Australia has become my home. I married an Aussie and eventually became an Australian citizen myself. While my roots are in Canada, my heart —and my work—are here. This unique blend of perspectives has shaped how I see the world, parenting, and the foster care system.

My husband, Sam and I have been in the foster care system for six years now. While that may seem like a short time in the grand scheme of things, it has been a journey of monumental highs and lows. Foster care is not for the faint of heart. It will excite you, fill you with love and compassion, and then break you, leaving you questioning if you have the strength to keep going. I don't say this to discourage you, but to be honest about the reality of the world of foster care. Despite the challenges, I wholeheartedly believe it is the most meaningful thing I'll ever do. However, that belief doesn't make the pain or struggles any less real.

My journey began when I was just a little girl. My upbringing wasn't perfect—nowhere near as challenging as what many of our foster kids endure, but not easy, either. At ten years old, I vividly remember telling a camp counsellor, while painting a little stool, that one day I would be a mum to kids who didn't have a mum. My parents often struggled to provide the emotional support I needed. That sense of emotional absence left a void, a longing to care for children who lacked the love and security of a stable family. I decided I'd have four biological kids and adopt eight more. That was my dream, though life has taken me on a different path.

This book shares my story, a journey filled with challenges, heartbreaks, and a desire for change within the foster care system. I'm writing to those who, like me, have chosen or found themselves in this world of fostering. Throughout my journey, I've searched high and low for books that could help me feel normal, as though someone out there understood my pain and struggles. I hope this book serves that purpose for others.

My path to creating a family has been anything but smooth. I'll delve into my experience with infertility and being childless, not by choice. I'll share my attempts to adopt in Australia, the highs and lows of temporary care, and the heartbreak of a placement breakdown. I'll also discuss the realities of caring for children in foster care, the emotional toll it takes, and the challenges of navigating Australia's foster care system. Balancing my role as a foster carer while spending time working within the foster care sector has given me a unique perspective on the system's bureaucratic and emotional complexities as well.

My hope is to see more children placed in loving homes. In Australia, many children are housed in hotel rooms or houses with youth workers instead of in families. This is not right. I've witnessed how hard it is to foster or adopt in this country. Too many potential carers are deterred by a system that seems insurmountably difficult. How many beautiful people are we losing as carers, and how many children are missing out on safe, secure homes because of these barriers?

I don't tell this story to shame anyone—individuals or organisations. This isn't a tale of "us versus them," carers against the system. No. This is about all of us—together—on the same team. We all want what's best for children in foster care. Yes, we may have different ideas about what that looks like, but I believe we can agree on one thing: the system needs to change. So, let's do this together—not in silos, not in isolation, not against each other. Let's stand side by side and work toward mending a system that has long been broken.

While this story is true, I've altered specific details to protect the privacy and safety of the children involved and my family. Foster care in Australia is a sensitive and complex field requiring utmost caution. I'll also address the complex topic of caring for Aboriginal and Torres Strait Islander people's children as a non-indigenous carer. While I don't claim to fully understand the history or experiences of Australia's Aboriginal and Torres Strait Islander people, I will share my perspective with respect and humility.

Throughout this book, I use the term "Aboriginal and Torres Strait Islander peoples" and "Aboriginal" to respectfully refer to the First Nations people of Australia. Aboriginal people are the original inhabitants of Australia, while Torres Strait Island people come from the Torres Strait Islands north of Queensland. Both groups have distinct cultures, languages and histories.

I can't possibly fit everything about foster care or our journey into a single book. There are experiences I didn't include, and some topics I couldn't fully explore here. If you find yourself left hanging, wanting more, or wondering why I didn't write about a particular situation—please know that it's not because it wasn't important. Some stories felt too fresh, too complex, or too private to share right now. Others simply didn't fit within the flow of this book. Writing about foster care—something so personal and layered—is a delicate process.

If you're curious to know more, or if this book touches something in you and leaves you with questions, I invite you to follow along as I continue to share in other ways. And if you feel safe to do so, please reach out. This book is a beginning, not a conclusion.

Every foster carer's journey is unique. I've spoken to carers whose experiences range from heartwarming to heartbreaking. Some receive a placement call within days of approval, while others grieve as long-term placements come to an end. For some, fostering is a straightforward process; for others, it's marked by frustration, pain, and systematic challenges.

If your journey has been relatively smooth, that's wonderful—it's how it should be. For those who feel bruised and battered by the system, I see you. While I haven't walked your exact path, I understand the pain and grief the journey can cause. I hope this book reminds you that you are not alone and inspires you to keep moving forward.

To the foster carer who's given up—I see you. I see your exhaustion, your heartbreak, your deep disappointment in a system that has let you down again and again. You've fought, you've tried, and you've held on longer than most could. And now, you feel like nothing will ever change.

I want you to know that your hopelessness is valid. You're not weak for feeling done—you're human. But I also want to show you something: that this work, this book—it all exists because I believe change *can* come. That your voice matters. That everything you've fought for hasn't been in vain. You may not have the strength right now to keep going, and that's okay. My hope is that, together, we can create something that brings you back to hope again.

If you're considering fostering, I encourage you to keep thinking about it. Maybe you don't have children but long to be a parent, or perhaps your children are older, and you have love to spare. The need for carers is immense, and while foster care is challenging, it's also incredibly rewarding. Dive deep, take the plunge, and join this beautiful, chaotic world of foster care.

This book is a deeply personal exploration of the highs and lows of foster care, framed by my journey as a foster carer. From the pain of infertility and the heartbreak of placement breakdowns to the resilience needed to navigate systemic challenges, each chapter reflects a different part of this complex experience. Along the way, I share stories of love, loss, and growth—not just mine, but also the children and carers who have crossed my path. It's a narrative about finding purpose in uncertainty, embracing the temporary, and holding on to hope amidst the chaos. Through it all, I hope to inspire, encourage, and shed light on the realities of foster care and adoption, reminding others that even in the hardest moments, the impact of love and stability can be life-changing.

I also share about becoming a parent. We didn't get pregnant and start with one baby, which then matured into a toddler and then a child. We got three at once and then added a fourth soon after—four children in different stages of life, each carrying their own impacts of trauma. We skipped Parenting 101 and went straight to a master class. I thought we were totally prepared to become parents. We had waited so long. I had read every book possible. I was ready, or so I thought.

I soon realised that I had no idea what I was doing. I now understand better when people say, "You'll understand when you're a parent." There were many areas in which I believed I would excel in motherhood. But I quickly learned that being a full-time mum to kids in care is a whole different ball game.

We faced all the "normal" things of parenthood—the things everyone experiences—getting used to the lack of sleep, being overwhelmed, messing up, tantrums, dealing with in-laws, and so on. But we faced these normal things of parenthood in addition to the complexities of being foster parents. Things like navigating the system, building bonds with children who came from trauma, managing relationships with birth families, and constantly preparing ourselves for the possibility of goodbye.

The journey began with the simple desire to become a mum—full of love and anticipation. Yet, it was soon met with unexpected challenges. Instead of a straight line, it became a winding road of waiting, grief and lessons in resilience and hope.

INFERTILITY

Infertility is a silent, invisible journey. It feels like a loss—like you've lost everything—but there is nothing tangible to mourn. Your hands are empty, yet the world around you struggles to understand your pain. As I shared in the introduction, I've always dreamed of being a mum. At 18, I looked down at my tummy one afternoon and said to my friend, 'I think I'm born to be a mum,' to which she replied, 'Of course you are, we all are.' Her words felt so natural, so unquestionable, as though motherhood was a given. But what happens when that doesn't become your reality? What does it mean when everyone you know is posting ultrasounds for their family and friends to celebrate the anticipation of their new baby, and you're left alone, having an emotional breakdown every 28-30 days? For many women, the idea of carrying and nurturing a life feels central to their identity. The natural design of the human body suggests this, but what happens when that dream doesn't come true?

———

I FACED infertility alone for a long time. I didn't even share much with my husband, Sam, initially. All he knew was that I was a bit overly emotional for a few days each month, and then I'd regulate my emotions. I couldn't share my deep desire to be a mum. It felt childish and immature to be so affected by not falling pregnant quickly after our marriage. I thought he'd think less of me.

For those of us who long for children, childlessness is devastating. All I ever wanted was to be a mum, and now I'm left with this gaping hole where a child should be. You reach an age where everyone around you is becoming parents—it's just the natural progression of life. And when you're the only one in your friend group without a child, you start to feel you don't belong.

Conversations shift. Kids become central to small talk. Women share how easily they conceived, how they're planning their second, how effortless it all seems. One afternoon, a friend casually mentioned, "We have to try *not* to fall pregnant," she laughed. I forced a light giggle in response, masking the tightness in my chest. The unfairness of it all felt suffocating.

SAM and I tried to naturally fall pregnant for four years, but nothing happened. Eventually, I persuaded Sam to see a doctor, who referred us to a fertility specialist. After a bit of testing, this specialist found Sam had very minimal sperm count, and our only way of getting pregnant would be through the IVF procedure. I was prepared to begin IVF, but Sam was not. It was an unknown area that he wasn't thrilled to explore.

Adoption was always something I wanted to do. As Sam wasn't sure about starting IVF at the time, I began contacting adoption agencies. The first one I contacted said we probably weren't fit to start the adoption process, as we had only just learned about our inability to fall pregnant. I contacted a second one, but we were sad to find out they didn't cover our local area.

We knew that international adoption was financially out of reach for us. It felt like every path to parenthood had been blocked. I was crushed. The doors kept slamming shut, one after the other, and I found myself lost in the grief of it all. My heart ached with longing, with the unmet expectation of holding a child in my arms. I was drowning in disappointment.

IVF WAS our only way forward—the only tangible option I could see to create the family I so desperately wanted. But Sam's reservations made me nervous. Would he be willing to go through with it? Could I ask him to?

I had to. I needed to try.

"I know this is overwhelming," I admitted, "but can we at least explore it? Just see what it entails?"

He hesitated. I saw the reluctance in his eyes, the fear of the unknown. But he also saw me—the depth of my desire, the ache I carried. And so, despite his reservations, he agreed.

We started the process soon after. From the very first appointment, it was emotionally exhausting. The clinics were sterile, eerily quiet, and filled with women, each carrying their own burdens of hope and heartbreak.

I went to the first appointment alone—Sam was working. Walking into the waiting room, I felt small. The weight of it all settled heavily on my shoulders. After checking in, I sat in silence, trying to steady my nerves, surrounded by women whose eyes reflected my own mix of anxiety and longing.

"Danielle Murphy?"

A nurse called my name, and I followed her down the hall. The ultrasound room was cold and impersonal. A quick scan, then another walk—this time to the surgeon's office.

He was confident, clinical. He spoke about the process in a matter-of-fact tone, listing the medications, the injections, and the side effects. As he spoke, my eyes wandered to the wall behind him, covered in photographs of babies—success stories. Smiling faces of parents who had once sat where I was sitting.

Maybe one day, I'll be on that wall, I thought.

Then, just like that, the appointment was over. I left with a prescription for hormone injections and a vague sense of unease.

GIVING myself injections every day quickly became routine. I carried my cooler bag with me to work, tucking it into the staff fridge alongside everyone else's lunch. When the time came, I'd slip away to a quiet corner, press the needle into my stomach, and go on with my day.

At first, I didn't feel much different. But as the weeks went on, the emotional toll became undeniable. My moods swung wildly, my patience frayed, my emotions ran high. I was exhausted—mentally, physically, emotionally.

One afternoon, I was scrolling through Facebook when I saw a friend's ultrasound photo, announcing her second pregnancy. The jealousy hit me like a tidal wave. My chest tightened, and before I knew it, I was on the floor, sobbing.

"Why does it happen for everyone else except me?" I screamed into the empty room.

The grief was relentless.

AFTER FOUR WEEKS OF INJECTIONS, it was time for the egg retrieval. Sam dropped me off at the clinic, and I walked in alone, my stomach twisting with nerves. The nurse who greeted me was kind, her voice soft as she explained what would happen next.

The procedure itself was supposed to be routine, but during the surgery, they discovered severe endometriosis.

I woke up groggy, the doctor's words sinking in slowly.

"We need to address the endometriosis before we can proceed," he said.

Everything stopped.

I had prepared myself for pain, for setbacks, for disappointment. But this was excruciating in a way I hadn't anticipated. We had retrieved the eggs. They were there. And yet, I couldn't move forward.

I wanted to fight it, to beg them to implant them, anyway. But my body wasn't ready.

And so, we had to wait.

———

BEFORE YOU ENTER THE PROCESS, you believe that you just have to go through it, and you'll come out with a baby in the end. But unfortunately, IVF has no guarantees. I've come to realise this is true through my own experiences and the stories shared by many others I've spoken with. Many people I have talked to have done 10+ rounds of IVF and never had a successful pregnancy. For anyone going through that process, I'm sorry. Some people will get that miracle story—finally getting pregnant—while many, if not most, will not. Others are left emotionally wounded and without a child.

One evening, during this time, Sam and I were speaking with a friend over dinner, and she began to tell us about her friend who did multiple rounds of IVF with no success. She went on, "Then they had a pastor pray for them, and within weeks, they were delighted to be pregnant. They got their miracle baby," she shared.

My heart sank as I listened to her story. *Where was my miracle?* Night after night I cried out—praying, pleading—for one. I knew, deep down, I was made to be a mum, and I couldn't understand why this was happening to me.

———

AFTER WE DEALT with the endometriosis through surgery, the surgeon said we could go back to IVF. We had made three attempts to get my hormone levels right, eggs big enough to collect, and my body suitable to carry, but complications kept arising. My body was not responding the way it should. We collected and fertilised two eggs, which the specialist advised us to freeze and try to implant in the coming months, once my body seemed stable enough to carry.

It was such a challenging time. Our marriage was being tested; my emotions were all over the place, and our finances were strained. My mental health was taking a real toll.

Social situations were often unbearable. Baby showers became emotional minefields, and every pregnancy announcement on social media felt like a personal jab, even though I rationally knew it wasn't.

Passing expectant mothers in public left me feeling raw. Each encounter served as a reminder of what I was missing, deepening the isolation and pain I felt.

MENTAL HEALTH around infertility is not straightforward. Mental health itself is a complex issue, and society as a whole is still learning to understand and address its many facets. Infertility compounds the complexity of mental health, intertwining physical, emotional, and societal factors. I believe much of my own mental health struggles stemmed from my infertility. During this time, I sought help the only way I knew how—by going to a GP for support. I shared my struggles with my emotions, anxieties about the future and relational challenges.

The GP gave me a response that was reductive—he labelled my experiences as a general anxiety disorder without acknowledging the underlying pain and circumstances that I was in. But how could he after a 15-minute appointment? At the time, I didn't have a deep understanding of the implications of infertility on mental health, so I just accepted his diagnosis and felt the shame of not being able to manage my emotions better.

Infertility isn't just a medical condition; it's a deeply personal journey that affects every aspect of life. The physical toll of treatments, the emotional weight of hope and disappointment, the financial burden, and the societal norms. Despite these challenges, the profound impact of infertility on mental health is often underestimated or misunderstood.

During my journey, I battled both anxiety and depression. It felt like a constant cycle of hope followed by crushing disappointment. I internalised the struggle. I thought, "What's wrong with me? Why can't I do what so many others seem to achieve so easily?" This internal dialogue became a spiral of hopelessness and shame.

Neither I nor those around me, including my husband and GP, fully recognised the impact infertility was having on my mental health. Doctors approached my symptoms in isolation, prescribing medication for anxiety without delving into the root causes. I now believe that a more holistic approach—one that acknowledged the emotional toll of infertility—would have made a significant difference in how I coped.

Looking back, I wish I had better understood the mental health implications of infertility. I wish there had been more open conversations, both in medical settings and among family and friends. If someone had said, "Your feelings are valid. This pain is real, and you're not alone," it could have eased the burden and helped me navigate those dark moments.

For anyone walking this path, I want you to know that it's okay to struggle. It's okay to grieve. Infertility is not just a physical condition—it's a journey that reshapes your identity, relationships, and dreams. Seeking support, whether through counselling, support groups, or connecting with others who've been there, can make all the difference.

IN THE END, IVF didn't give us the child we had hoped for. It did, however, shape me in ways I couldn't have anticipated. It taught me resilience, deepened my empathy, and ultimately guided me toward a different path to motherhood. Though my arms remained empty, my heart was being prepared for a different story.

Infertility is still a part of our lives. Just because we chose to go down the path of adoption and foster care doesn't mean that area is gone. Many times over the following years, I questioned our decision not to pursue IVF further. We still had to grapple with the idea that we would never hold our own biological child in our arms. We didn't make the choice lightly, but we decided to close the door on getting pregnant permanently, with me having a hysterectomy. There is no going back. On one hand, I'm grateful I'm not reminded monthly that I'm not pregnant, and on the other, I still get reminded of the grief when I think about our situation without permanent children in our care.

BEFORE I GO on to speak about our adoption and fostering journey. I want to clarify that adoption and fostering cannot fill the hole of your infertility. If that is your goal, you will be very disappointed. Yes, being a mother to a child is an amazing experience, but mothering a child from foster care is very different from being a mother to your own biological child. There will be many things you will need to accept and change that differ from parenting your own child. I do not want to deter anyone unable to have a biological child from considering fostering or adopting, but it is paramount that they understand the complexities they will face, as we did, and ensure they are ready to accept the difference.

On the other hand, some may try to deter you from foster care because you haven't had a child of your own. While I understand their concerns, I believe that people who have faced infertility have so much to offer children in care and shouldn't be denied the opportunity. With the right support and preparation, they can be incredible foster carers. It not only provides a loving home for a child but also fulfils the childless person's lifelong dream of offering love and care.

If you're walking through infertility, I want you to feel seen. This is hard. This is heavy. Grief comes in waves and is rarely neat and tidy. However, your next chapter looks—continuing treatment, fostering, adoption, or choosing to stop—feel everything you feel and know you're not alone.

―――

AT THIS POINT in our journey, we had two frozen embryos. The doctor told us we could move forward with an implantation if we were ready. I went in for one final ultrasound. Lying on the now very familiar exam table, the nurse studied the screen carefully before offering a reassuring smile. "Everything looks great," she said. "We can proceed with the implantation in a week." Hope flickered inside me as we booked the procedure. A week. Seven more days of waiting in anticipation, and then we would finally be parents.

Yes, I Want to Adopt!

We had a few more days left before the embryo implantation surgery. Sam and I went for lunch at our favourite local restaurant, and my phone rang with an unknown number.

It was the adoption agency we had contacted twelve months earlier. They said they had made a clerical error when they last spoke with us. They had previously told us we were not in their coverage area, but they realised their mistake and *did* cover our area. We were excited when they asked if we would consider adopting a sibling group. "Of course!" I replied.

Later that night, Sam and I discussed the decision. "Would you rather have two children who are not biologically yours or one child who is biologically yours. But you cannot pursue adoption until your biological child is 5 years old?" Sam asked me. That was the policy the agency told us concerning adoption.

It wasn't an overly tough decision at the time. We both agreed we would rather adopt a sibling group than have a child of our own. This would mean stopping IVF. For me, my desire was always to be a mum, and it didn't matter to me if they were biologically mine or not.

THE NEXT MORNING, I picked up the phone and called the IVF clinic. My heart pounded as I listened to the line ring, but I steadied myself.

"I need to cancel our appointment for the implantation," I said.

There was a pause. "Are you sure?" the receptionist asked gently.

"Yes," I replied, my voice firm. "I'll call when we're ready to rebook."

But deep down, I knew I wouldn't. I wouldn't need to. We were going to adopt soon. I was certain of it. This was the right path. The one that would finally make me a mum.

We waited for the agency to attend our home for our information session. The meeting took place, and he gave us the information and application paperwork. We were both ready to get started. I filled out the application documents in record time and dropped them off at the agency.

NOTHING HAPPENED FOR SIX MONTHS, and then we attended the mandatory training.

We were hopeful that now that we had completed the training, we would begin our assessments soon. Unfortunately, it was another ten months before we had our first assessment meeting. During this period, we were impatient. We would see social media posts about the 45,000 children who need a forever home in Australia, yet we were still waiting. We pestered the agency often, hoping for some movement. Finally, they called to book our first assessment meeting.

The assessment process was both exciting and deeply invasive, like peeling back the layers of our lives for someone else to scrutinise. I had expected tough questions, but I hadn't anticipated just how vulnerable it would make me feel.

Some questions were easy to answer, but others left me unsettled, forcing me to confront parts of myself I preferred to keep private. They probed deeply into my mental health—an area I felt confident in managing—yet their scrutiny made me second-guess myself. They asked about my childhood trauma. Something I had long accepted wasn't my fault, yet in that moment, it felt like a mark against me, a burden I still had to carry. Our financial position, which we had felt secure in, was picked apart and analysed as if stability wasn't enough—it had to be proven beyond a doubt.

Each session stretched for two to three hours, a slow and exhausting excavation of our lives. We laid everything bare—our infertility struggles, mental health, the intricacies of our marriage. It was necessary; I understood that. But it also left me wondering —how much of myself would I have to justify before we were deemed worthy?

At one point in the assessment process, they separated Sam and me for individual interviews. It felt a bit like an interrogation, though I knew it was just another step in proving we were fit to be parents. One of the questions was blunt. "Has either of you ever physically hurt the other?"

I didn't hesitate. "No."

But in Sam's interview, he hesitated just long enough. He was never one to lie, and while neither of us had crossed a serious line, there was one moment—one that still made my stomach twist with regret.

It had been years ago, in the middle of an argument that had spiralled out of control. I don't even remember what it was about, only the white-hot frustration that boiled over. In that moment, I grabbed the nearest thing—an empty glass—and hurled it in his direction. I hadn't aimed to hit him, and thankfully, I didn't. But the sound of it shattering against the wall had been enough to startle us both into silence.

It was a stupid, impulsive mistake. One I never repeated. One I wished I could take back.

BEFORE I GO ON, I want to note something important here. As I was getting feedback from others about this book, someone told me maybe I shouldn't include this story in the book. "It might be used against you," they said. And they're right—it makes me look bad. It makes me look human.

If you've never lost your temper, never said something you regret, never done something in a moment of pain or stress that you wish you could take back, then by all means, judge me. But I don't think you'll find many people who have walked through life without these moments.

I'm not saying we excuse unhealthy behaviour, but we do need to be honest about the emotional toll this life takes. If we expect perfection from foster carers, we'll lose them. We need to allow room for people to be flawed and still worthy of doing this work. One mistake doesn't define a person. If it did, none of us would be here. And that's why I kept this story in here—even though I risk judgement—because people need to allow foster carers to be human, not expect perfection.

WHEN SAM later told me he had shared it with the assessors, my heart sank. We had agreed to be honest, but I hadn't thought about how that honesty might be received. And I was right to worry.

What had been a single regrettable moment in our marriage quickly unravelled into a thread the agency couldn't ignore. More questions. More scrutiny. More hoops to jump through before we could gain approval.

I understood why they had to be cautious. They were trying to protect vulnerable children. But at that moment, it felt like I was being judged not for the mother I could be, but for the worst version of myself—the person I had been for a fleeting, fractured second in time.

We knew our marriage was strong. We had faced numerous challenges together and emerged more resilient each time. But convincing the assessors of this was exhausting. Their scrutiny was relentless. In the end, I had to consult a psychologist and obtain a letter of recommendation to demonstrate my emotional stability, even though I had already shared my past therapy sessions and my willingness to seek help whenever needed.

It wasn't the act of seeing a psychologist that was difficult; it was the constant need to prove ourselves over and over again. That persistent questioning of our worthiness made an already taxing process feel almost insurmountable.

We sent off the last of our required documents, exhaling a breath we hadn't realised we'd been holding. After months of scrutiny, interviews, and endless paperwork, all we could do now was wait.

Thankfully, our assessors saw the good in us. They believed in our ability to provide a safe and loving home and advocated for our approval.

―――

THEN, one afternoon, my phone rang. I recognised the number instantly and felt my stomach tighten. I hesitated for just a moment before answering.

"Hello?"

Our caseworker's voice came through, brimming with excitement.

"You've been approved!"

Relief flooded through me. I barely registered what she said next—something about receiving the official paperwork soon—because at that moment, all that mattered was that we had made it. We were officially foster carers with a view to adopt.

From our very first inquiry to panel approval, the process stretched over twenty-eight months—two and a half years of waiting, hoping, and proving ourselves. And yet, even after finally being approved, there was still more waiting to be done.

We had been open to various backgrounds and were approved for a sibling group of three. "You'll get lots of calls for matches right away," they assured us. I clung to that promise, desperate for the moment when we'd finally hear, *This is it. These are your kids.*

JUST ONE WEEK LATER, my phone rang. My heart pounded as I answered.

"We have two Aboriginal boys in need of a permanent placement. Would you consider it?"

I hesitated. The words *permanent placement* made my pulse quicken—but I knew what it meant. Because they were Aboriginal, adoption would never be an option for us. It also wasn't a sibling group of three, and throughout the process, we had heard heartbreaking stories of large sibling groups being separated because no one could take them all. That reality had weighed on us. We were approved for three children and had always envisioned opening our home to a larger sibling set, keeping them together.

I wanted to say yes so badly. I wanted a match. I wanted to be a mum. But something inside me whispered that this wasn't the right yes.

We took time to think it through, but the answer didn't change. With a heavy heart, I called the caseworker back. "I don't think this is the right match for us," I told her. "We're hoping to take in a larger sibling group."

She wasn't surprised. "I understand," she said. "I'll be in touch when another match comes through."

The next week passed, then another. The anticipation was suffocating. Then, finally, the phone rang again.

I held my breath as I answered.

"We have a match for four children. Would you consider it?"

"Of course!" I blurted out without hesitation.

The caseworker chuckled but quickly added, "There's just

one thing—you're only approved for three children. You'd need additional approval for a fourth."

That didn't scare me. We had waited so long for this moment. I would do whatever it took.

"We'll do whatever we need to," I assured her.

I hung up the phone, my hands trembling. After years of waiting, hoping, and heartbreak, it was finally happening.

I was going to be a mum.

WITHIN A FEW WEEKS, we met them in person.

We arrived at the temporary carers' house, buzzing with a mix of excitement and nerves. "I feel like I'm going to vomit," I said to Sam with a shaky grin. We stepped onto the veranda and knocked on the door. The carer greeted us warmly, and the caseworker was there, too, ushering us inside.

The children were sitting in the lounge room, having afternoon tea. We smiled and said hello before following the carer and caseworker into the kitchen. It all felt surreal.

We introduced ourselves and chatted with the carers for a while. They filled us in on the children a little, then brought us into the lounge room for formal introductions.

The eldest, Jenny, was seven. Though small in stature, she had the sharp eyes and steady presence of a protector, always watching out for her younger brothers. Next was five-year-old Jonny, quiet and gentle, with a sweetness that shone through in every interaction. A little encouragement lit him up. Then came Jared, three years old, bursting with energy and mischief, but never too busy for a cuddle. And finally, James. At two years old, he was a chubby, cheerful toddler, happily babbling as he explored the world around him.

"Hi, I'm Dani, and this is Sam," I said.

"Hey, guys!"

They showed us their toys with pride, and little James quickly pulled Sam over to read him a story. Jenny was drawing at the table and, a few moments later, proudly held up her picture to show us. We spent time playing with them—bouncing on the trampoline, hearing all about their day, laughing, and soaking in the joy.

At one point, the carer gently pulled us aside to share more of their story. It was heartbreaking—like so many stories of children in care. These children had been through a lot. You could see it in their small frames and their malnourished bodies. But despite everything, they were happy. And they were beautiful.

They were perfect. Their personalities felt like puzzle pieces that fit right into our family. It felt as if it was meant to be. Sam and I fell for them completely—and we knew, without a doubt, we wanted them in our home as soon as possible.

WE KNEW that having four children would be a lot of work, and we had always made it clear to the agency that I would resign from my job to be a full-time mum to them. We were told it would only be a couple of months before a full-time move, so I resigned from my employment position and focused on preparing for their arrival.

As we got to know them, everything just fell into place. We got along so well. They loved coming to stay with us, and we were ready for them to be with us forever. But as I now know, the system is not quick, and just because it's "meant to be" doesn't mean it will be.

For six months, we have been getting to know the children—visiting them at their temporary carer's house, taking them to the park, and gradually spending more time together. What started as occasional visits soon became a structured routine, with us providing weekly respite care for two of the children, then quickly expanding to include all four.

In Australia, respite care typically gives foster carers a break—usually one weekend a month or as needed in urgent situations. However, in our case, respite served a different purpose: it was a bridge, a way to ease the children into the idea of being with us full-time.

The children didn't know we were being considered as their forever family. That part remained unspoken. But their temporary carer and we understood that this was the goal—to build trust, connection, and familiarity, so that when the time came, the transition would feel as natural as possible.

AS TIME WENT ON, the back-and-forth became harder. Whenever I dropped them back to their temporary carer, I cried. My heart was aching to have them with us forever, but I had to drop them back to a temporary carer with no certainty or timeline of how long the transition would go on for. The temporary carer would send me photos of the kids to try to keep us connected, but that often made it harder.

I just wanted the children in our home for good. They were meant to be with us full-time now, and with each day that passed, I felt like I was missing out. Knowing the children who were going to be placed with us, seeing them have new experiences with the temporary carer, and having to wait for the final placement, was all so hard.

We had expected they would be in our full-time care in December, and then it was moved to January, then March. Now, we were at the end of April, and there was no plan for when they would be with us full-time. Logically, I know it is just the reality of fostering to adopt. You miss out on many of the big milestones with the children. We will never get to see them when they were babies; we have missed seven birthdays of Jenny's. James just had his birthday, and instead of celebrating with us, he was still with his temporary carers.

It felt so unfair. I want to give a forever home to these four children, but we were stuck—waiting while the agency worked through its long list of procedures. *Is that just the way it has to be? Do they really need to follow these processes? Or is the frustration I feel a sign that things need to change?* My mind spun with questions I couldn't answer.

Trying to adopt from foster care was anything but easy. I had braced myself for challenges, but the reality was so much harder than I anticipated. Navigating the system was just the beginning—there were endless hurdles. The back-and-forth with temporary carers, the emotional weight of meeting birth family members, and the relentless uncertainty of the process. It wasn't just about what we had to give the children—it was about everything we had to navigate.

THE CHILDREN WERE STILL LIVING with their temporary carers, but we were still seeing them regularly. Then came Jonny's sixth birthday party—a moment that brought the realities of adopting from foster care into sharp focus.

I'd been looking forward to the party, imagining how special we could make Jonny feel and how we could show him he was loved. The day arrived, and we stepped into the backyard, where the celebration was already underway. Jonny saw us first. His face lit up with the kind of smile that could melt anyone's heart. Then Jenny, his older sister, bounded over to us, excitement spilling out as she said, "Mum's here! I want you to meet her."

We hadn't been told their birth mother would be there. My stomach churned with nerves, but I forced a smile and followed Jenny's lead. She was polite but brief, her attention elsewhere. I shrugged it off and turned my focus to chatting with the other guests, trying to hide the anxiety I felt.

To one side of the yard, two men sat on a bench, apart from the crowd. Jenny, instead of running around with the other kids, sat with them. Curious, we eventually learned they were the children's grandfather and step-grandfather. Jenny introduced them as "Pop and Pop." Despite their rough edges, their warmth shone through. They reminded me of the men I'd worked with during my time in homelessness services—kind souls weathered by life's storms.

The day was filled with moments like these—bits of joy mixed with a profound heaviness. Their mother was trying to rebuild her life after losing her children to an abusive relationship, and I could see the weight she carried. When everyone sang "Happy Birthday" to Jonny, his mother's eyes filled up with tears. It was the kind of pain that hung heavy in the air—the pain of wanting to fulfil the role of a mother but knowing it was out of reach. My heart ached for her.

Throughout the party, I observed Jared, the younger middle child. At just three, his worlds were colliding with a force no child should endure. His birth mother, his temporary carer, and me—his prospective adoptive mother—all in the same space. He went between play and uncertainty, never fully settling with any of us. It was as though he couldn't decide where he belonged.

When it was time to leave, Jared had melted into a full-blown tantrum. His temporary carer brought him to me, and I scooped him into my arms, rocking him gently. My heart clenched as I held him—this child who was just beginning to find safety in me, yet still carried so much confusion and pain. Eventually, I encouraged him to seek comfort from his mother. He hesitated, but went.

By the time we said our goodbyes, I was running on fumes. My body was screaming for rest. As soon as we got home, I collapsed onto the couch, my mind swirling with anxiety and my stomach knotted with nausea.

This was the reality of adopting from foster care, though. It wasn't just about paperwork and waiting; it was about stepping into the complex, messy, complicated lives of children and their families. And it was hard—harder than I ever imagined.

EASTER WEEKEND ROLLED AROUND, and the temporary carer sent me some photos of the kids doing an Easter egg hunt.

As soon as I saw those photos, my heart dropped, and my eyes filled with tears. "I'm supposed to be the one planning the Easter egg hunt. I'm the one who should be spoiling them with chocolates and making those memories," I thought.

At this point, we were fully invested in the children, but we still needed approval to take in all four of them. We had already jumped through every hoop they put in front of us, yet the demands kept coming.

One of the latest requirements? A calendar.

"A calendar?" I scoffed, throwing my hands up in frustration. "Do they think we're idiots?"

Sam shook his head. "This is ridiculous. Of course, we know we'll need to be organised with four kids. And how are we supposed to plan a schedule when we don't even know what their appointments will be?"

It felt like just another box to tick, another pointless task standing between us and the family we so desperately wanted. But we did it anyway.

We had already done everything they asked—interviews, paperwork, assessments. Yet, it never seemed to be enough. The frustration was mounting, but our determination outweighed our exhaustion. We wanted these kids too much to stop now.

ADOPTION BEGAN WITH SUCH EXCITEMENT. We put aside having our own children through IVF, hopeful that instead of one child of our own, we would soon have forever children through adoption. The match seemed perfect, and everything felt like fate at first, but then, as things unfolded, it all began to fall apart.

The Breaking Point

After months of proving ourselves capable of caring for four children, we finally received approval to take in a sibling group of four. One would think we'd be overjoyed, but instead, I felt deflated. While it was an answer to prayer and a significant step forward, I couldn't shake the exhaustion and frustration from the journey to get here. This pain could have been avoided months ago. The process wore me down, and I was tired—tired of constantly proving myself, tired of feeling unheard, and tired of fighting to make others do the right thing.

Yes, I was grateful for the approval. But I wished it hadn't come at such a high cost—our sanity and precious time with the children. The excitement of welcoming four children we deeply loved was overshadowed by the relentless policies and procedures the agency required us to follow. It felt as if the system, rather than being a support, was an obstacle we had to endure.

Even as we grappled with uncertainty, we remained fully committed to becoming the forever family for these children. We had the approval to care for four, and we held onto hope that it wouldn't be much longer before they were with us full-time.

DURING THIS TIME, an unexpected reminder of our past surfaced—a bill for the frozen embryos we had stored. It wasn't cheap. Sam and I sat down to discuss it.

"Do we keep paying for it, or do we let them go?" he asked. "Are we going to try again?"

He wasn't pushing me one way or another—just making space for my feelings. He had always made sure my desires were heard in this process, knowing how deeply I wanted to be a mother.

I sat on the floor in my office, the weight of the decision pressing down on me. The embryo storage form lay in front of me, a stark reminder of a future that once felt certain. I traced my fingers over the paper, reading the options again and again, even though I already knew what it said. My mind wandered to what could have been—the road I had once been so determined to take.

But deep down, I already knew. All I wanted was to be a mother to these four children. I didn't need a biological child; with them in my life, I already felt complete.

So, I signed the papers, deciding to donate the embryos to science. A friend had to co-sign, and when she hesitated, questioning my certainty, I reassured her. I was confident—so sure I was making the right decision.

And yet, as time passed, I found myself regretting it. Strangely enough though—deep down—I still believe it was the right decision.

A COUPLE OF WEEKS LATER, we received a request from the agency. They needed us to do respite care again because the current carer couldn't manage Jonny's behaviours.

The request brought up our frustrations. We knew deep down it wasn't Jonny's fault. This child was yearning for a forever family, and the prolonged process was only compounding his pain. Yet, it felt like our concerns were ignored. At the time, I was frustrated. I judged the temporary carer harshly. I remember thinking, *how could she not know how to manage him properly? Why wasn't she doing all the trauma-informed strategies we had learned in training?*

But I know now that I was being unfair. Yes, she wasn't following every trauma-informed practice by the book, but I've since learned that in the chaos of fostering, no one does—at least not all the time. Sometimes, you have to survive. You make the best choices you can in the moment, even if they're not in exact alignment with the training.

I see now that she was probably overwhelmed, just as I was. I was so focused on what she wasn't doing that I failed to see how hard she was trying. Experience has a way of humbling you.

Without a clear timeline for the children's transition to permanent care with us, we were hesitant to step in and do respite again. We wanted to see the children again, but we wanted them to be with us full-time and believed the prolonged process was unnecessary. A part of us wanted to say no—hoping it would force the agency to make a definite decision about the transition.

We sent a firm email outlining our conditions. We would take the children, but wanted a clear timeline of when they would move in with us. We proposed moving all four children during the upcoming school holidays, a solution that made sense for everyone involved. The weight of the situation lingered with me as we waited for their response. The agency's response wasn't what we hoped for. They couldn't provide us with a clear timeline, and the path that seemed logical and straightforward to us, wasn't the direction they wanted to take.

We pushed back once more, saying we couldn't do any more respite until the children were permanently placed with us. The constant back-and-forth was taking a toll on us and the kids. But the agency returned with another plea. They needed us to take Jonny for respite because the carer wasn't coping. If we declined, they warned, Jonny would be sent to another temporary carer for a few nights. My heart ached at the thought. Jonny had already endured so much instability, and this would only deepen his wounds.

We wrestled with the decision. Saying yes felt like we might be overlooking the agency's struggle to manage the situation effectively. After all, if they had moved the kids when we first suggested it, this entire issue could have been avoided. But saying no meant Jonny would be uprooted again, and the thought of him facing yet another disruption broke me.

Desperate for guidance, we called a foster care support line. They advised us to take the respite, explaining it would show the agency we were ready and willing for the permanent move. Reluctantly, we agreed—but with conditions. We insisted on having all four children for the five-night respite and a firm date for the matching meeting. To our surprise, the agency agreed.

Excitement and nerves tangled within me. I loved having the children with us, but returning them afterwards was agony. Dropping them back each time felt like abandoning them. I wanted nothing more than to shield and protect them. However, it felt like the agency was failing to provide the stability they deserved by moving them in with us permanently.

The five-night respite went ahead, and the agency promised to confirm the date for the next matching meeting soon. However, "soon" in their language often translates to an indefinite wait. Despite the absurdity of needing another matching meeting—after eight months of saying yes to this match—we had no choice but to comply. We pushed back slightly, asking for a solid date, but were met with vague promises of a decision within the next couple of weeks.

Their carer dropped them off in the morning for respite, and I spent the first few hours at home with them. Transition days were always the hardest, but this one made it painfully clear—these children needed to get into their permanent home as soon as possible.

Jonny was defiant, pushing every boundary. He always tested limits, but today was different—more intense, more desperate. The other kids had full meltdowns within the hour. I did my best to stay present, to be emotionally available, and slowly, they responded. By the next day, they were noticeably calmer, settling back into themselves while in our care. The contrast was undeniable.

DURING THIS FIVE-NIGHT RESPITE, I had a specialist appointment to discuss my endometriosis and how to manage the symptoms. Sam took the older three to the park while I brought the littlest one, James, with me to the office. Sitting across from the physician, I explained the chronic pain, the failed treatments, and the exhaustion of trying to manage it all. He listened, nodding as I spoke, then finally said what I had been fearing but also expecting— "A hysterectomy is probably your best option."

He hesitated. "You're young," he said carefully, "and this is a permanent decision."

I had already considered that. "We're adopting these four kids," I explained. "We've made the decision not to have biological kids of our own."

That seemed to reassure him. He laid out my options— waiting for a public system surgery, which could take up to twelve months, or exploring private options for a sooner date. He left the decision in my hands.

Later, I brought the information back to Sam. His concern was immediate. "Another twelve months of this pain?" he said, frustration in his voice. "I hate watching you go through this."

We sat with it, knowing a decision had to be made, but not ready to make it just yet. So we shelved the conversation, turned our focus back to the kids, and soaked up the last few days with them.

AND THEN, all too soon, it was time to take them back to their temporary carer.

The behaviours began again. Jenny said she didn't want to go back to the carers but wanted more nights at our place; Jared lost it while we drove to the carers; James said he didn't want to go back and screamed for cuddles from me. It was so hard seeing our little kids crying because they wanted to stay. It was evident from their behaviour that they were longing for a family of their own. We wanted so badly to say they could stay with us forever, but we couldn't.

We again went back to the agency and said we didn't want to do respite until it was a permanent move because it was too hard on the kids. With a matching meeting in a couple of weeks, we had to wait till then to figure out the plan moving forward.

It deeply saddened me that it had come to this. Once again, I was reminded of just how challenging this process is—and it's no surprise there are so many children waiting for forever families in Australia. At this point, I find it hard to recommend this process to anyone.

WHEN WE WERE WAITING, we often wondered if we needed to prepare more. But how much more could we do? We had already prepared in every way we could think of—again and again—until preparing started to feel pointless.

We renovated our first house to make it perfect for kids, only to move before we were matched. We poured ourselves into our new home, installing a playground, a sandpit, fences, bunk beds, toys, and every child-related essential we could think of. And yet, we were still waiting. How much more could we possibly do?

Ironically, in some ways, we feel less prepared now than we were when we first received the match. When we first got the match, we were in a solid financial position. Now, we're not. I haven't worked in eight months, because we were supposed to have kids by now. We structured our lives around the expectation that we'd have children placed with us soon, that I'd be home parenting while agency funds supplemented our income. We made sacrifices, we adjusted our plans, we put everything on hold —because the children were coming "soon".

And yet, nearly three years later, we still don't have children in our home full-time.

Even though we have said "yes" to these kids repeatedly for the past eight months, the agency needed to do an official placement meeting. This meeting was part of their process to sit down with us and go through more of the children's files, and for us to make an official decision whether we wanted to say yes to this match. We were given all the information for the kids. History, medical, family dynamics, needs, etc. We went into the meeting with no concerns about the kids and came out of the meeting with no concerns about the kids. Our biggest concern wasn't about the children themselves—we were wholeheartedly committed to them. Our worry was the never-ending length of the process and the uncertainty surrounding their transition into our home.

The agency repeatedly told us they couldn't move the kids while they were still under temporary care orders. Yet, in the same breath, they informed us that a matching meeting was scheduled for the following week to discuss moving them on temporary orders. It was baffling. We had heard from other foster carers that, in most cases, agencies do move children under temporary orders when it suits their timeline, but now, when it was about our match, they were saying it wasn't possible.

We felt stuck in a cycle of conflicting information. Were we being strung along? Was this just another delay in a process that had already dragged on for far too long? Or was this truly a legal restriction they couldn't work around? At this point, we didn't know what to believe, and that uncertainty made the wait even harder.

We had said yes to these children in October, understanding that they would be placed with us around December. Then it moved to the beginning of the new year. But now, months later, that promise felt like a distant illusion.

"Why did they even bring us this match?" Sam asked, frustration evident in his voice. I met his gaze, mirroring his disbelief.

"I don't know," I admitted. "If I had known it would take another year just to move forward, I might never have agreed."

And yet, here we were, months later, still in limbo. There was no guarantee that all four children would be in our care anytime soon. We had spent so much time waiting for decisions, waiting for movement, waiting for something to change. But the system moved at its own pace. We felt like they were indifferent to the emotional toll it took on us and, more importantly, on the children.

WHILE I STILL BELIEVE THAT the system moves far too slowly and inefficiently for children in care, I've come to appreciate that there were good people genuinely trying to make this placement happen. Our caseworker, for one, was incredible. I remember standing outside of our home with her one afternoon, discussing the situation. She empathised with us deeply, acknowledging how hard it had been. "I'd place five children with you tomorrow if I could," she said with sincerity. It was reassuring to know that the delay wasn't a reflection of our capability—it was simply part of the drawn-out process.

AS WE APPROACHED the middle of the year, we still had no clear timeline. At this rate, it felt like it could drag out another 12 months—or even longer. The thought was unbearable.

There was talk about one moving in with us. However, the others were to remain in their temporary carers' house until the end of the year.

"What?" I turned to Sam, stunned. "Are they serious? They want to split them up? What if they only place two of them with us?" My heart was pounding. "We can't separate them—not again."

They had already been split up once when they first entered

care, and the effects were still so evident. Especially in Jenny, the oldest. She carried the weight of it on her small shoulders. Even a temporary separation—six to twelve months—would crush her. We couldn't do that to them. Not after everything.

We had lost all hope in the agency and in the process.

We thought the agency's goals would be aligned with ours—that if they wanted us to have these children, they would work with us to make it happen as soon as possible. We were wrong. The agency seemed more focused on ticking boxes and following every policy and protocol to the letter, even when those protocols didn't make sense for this situation, these children, or us.

I felt like we had lost. We had been given a precious window to impact these children's lives, and that window was closing fast. My mind spun with worries about their development, about the critical moments they were missing, and about the ripple effects this would have on their futures. The early years are the most critical in a child's life. In my mind, providing them with the stability of a family as soon as possible was essential. At times, though, it felt like the agency was more focused on following procedures than on creating a sense of home, family and belonging for the children.

No matter how loudly we raised our concerns, no one with the power to act seemed to be listening. Friends and colleagues outside the situation agreed with us—they could see the flaws in how things were being handled—but within the agency, it seemed as though our words fell on deaf ears.

I began questioning everything. Had we missed our chance? Was it too late to make a difference for these children? I told myself we had done all we could, and that the failure wasn't ours, but the doubt gnawed at me. I needed someone to tell me it wasn't hopeless, that we hadn't missed the window. But that reassurance never came.

WE FOUND OURSELVES AT A CROSSROADS. Upper management was pushing back on placing all four children with us, despite everything we had done to prove ourselves. We had been approved for a sibling group of four, yet they hesitated, questioning whether moving them all in together was the right decision. Their plan was to place one child first, possibly a second in six months, and then reassess the remaining two.

But that didn't sit right with us.

"Will they ever place the other two with us?" Sam asked, his voice edged with frustration.

"What if they don't?" I responded, the weight of that possibility sinking in.

The thought of the children being separated indefinitely filled us with anger. How could they justify this? How could they expect us to take in some of the siblings while leaving the others behind, with no certainty they would ever join us? It wasn't just a logistical nightmare—it was emotional cruelty, both for us and for the children who deserved stability and to stay together. We had consistently demonstrated our ability to care for all four children —it was never a question of capacity. Time and again, we documented how we managed and shared those details with the agency. Our caseworker praised our capability and the way we handled the challenges.

"This is ridiculous," Sam muttered, running a hand through his hair. I could see the same frustration burning in his eyes that I felt in my chest.

We weren't just upset—we were furious. Furious at the senselessness of a system that seemed to create more barriers than solutions. Furious at the agency's lack of urgency. Furious that, once again, we were left feeling powerless while the children's future dangled in uncertainty.

Desperate for clarity, we reached out to the child protection office on the advice of a friend in the field, hoping for guidance. Instead, it backfired. The agency found out and became defensive, digging their heels in even further. What had started as a plea for help only escalated the tension.

Determined not to let things unravel, we requested a meeting with management, hoping—praying—for a resolution.

When the meeting was called, we entered the room with heavy hearts and frayed nerves. It felt more like a courtroom than a collaboration. We laid out our case as calmly and clearly as we could. We explained our concerns, our commitment, and how splitting the siblings would irreparably damage their bond and their sense of safety.

The agency seemed more focused on reprimanding us for calling child safety for support than truly listening. They cited policies, timelines, and their own limitations, but none of them addressed what mattered most to us—the well-being of the children. Ten months earlier, they had promised us a forever family with these kids. Yet now, we were in the impossible position of fighting to keep them together.

As I tried to explain, my tears betrayed me. I couldn't hold back the sobs as I poured out my heart. "How can I be the one responsible for hurting these children by separating them?" I asked, my voice cracking under the weight of the situation. "How could you expect us—the very people who were ready to be their parents—to take some and leave the others behind?"

Even if it was temporary, the emotional damage would be devastating, not just for the children, but for us, too. The thought of rejecting even one of them felt unbearable. These weren't just names on a case file; they were siblings, a family, and they deserved to stay that way.

Despite our pleas, the agency workers remained committed to their processes and weren't willing to explore the alternatives we proposed. I could see that one worker in particular was genuinely trying to keep the children together, and I appreciated her commitment. But we found ourselves clashing—not in intent, but on what the child's best interest looked like in practice. While we shared the same goal, we had very different views on how to get there.

They continued to raise another concern. "You mentioned you were thinking of moving. Can you explain?"

From the very beginning, we had been upfront with the agency, letting them know we might move one day—to be closer to family. They had reassured us this wouldn't be a problem at all. But now, in this meeting, everything changed.

"You can't move with these kids," they stated firmly. "Their cases are too complex, and the paperwork will be lost."

"What?!" I thought, completely blindsided. I sat there in shock, trying to process what they had just said. How could they suddenly change their stance? They had told us before that moving wouldn't be an issue. It felt like a betrayal—another broken promise—and it left us scrambling to figure out our next steps.

This was yet another example of the agency's persistent lack of transparency and communication. Time and time again, they withheld critical information, only to reveal it when it was too late to adjust our plans.

EVEN AS A WORKER myself at different foster care agencies, I have seen the same frustrations from the inside. Upper management often operates with a "need-to-know" mentality, making decisions behind closed doors and leaving caseworkers, their own staff, and carers in the dark. The lack of clear communication trickles down, causing confusion and damaging trust at every level.

I would relay information to carers in good faith, only to return to the office and be told that management had changed its decision. It was infuriating. Not only did it make me appear dishonest, but it also reinforced the deep-rooted issue: agencies don't communicate transparently.

WE WERE STILL HOLDING out hope that our forever children would move in permanently soon, but in the meantime, we also did respite care for other foster children, and I genuinely enjoyed it. It gave us little windows into the lives of so many children, each one carrying a story more complex than the last. One Friday afternoon, around 4 p.m., the manager of the agency called.

"Hey Dani, there's a nine-year-old girl named Jess who needs a last-minute respite placement. Her current temporary carer is away for training, and her intended respite placement just fell through. Would you be able to take her?"

Of course, we could.

We had about an hour to get ready before we needed to be on the road. We quickly showered and packed the car, then drove the 45 minutes into the city to pick her up. The woman who opened the door was Martha, a retired teacher in her sixties who'd been fostering kids temporarily for decades. She welcomed us warmly and offered us a cup of tea, which we gratefully accepted.

Jess was curled up with an iPad, half-watching something but clearly listening. She peeked around the corner and gave us a quiet, polite "hello." Martha's home was well-worn, dim, cluttered, and filled with the weight of years and stories—she, herself, was kind and grounded. We sat and chatted about Jess and her experience in the foster care system. Jess's belongings were already packed in a small bag. Before we left, Martha asked Jess for a kiss on the cheek. Jess obliged a little shyly, and we were on our way.

In the car, Jess came to life. She talked the entire way home about her family, the music she loved, and what she hoped her weekend would be like. We turned up some pop songs, and soon she was belting out the lyrics, the wind from the open window brushing her face like freedom.

When we got home, I gave her a quick tour. She lit up at the sight of the dogs and the toy shelf, and when she noticed our keyboard, her eyes went wide.

"You have a piano!" she gasped and ran over to it.

That night, we played Monopoly Deal and UNO. Around 7:30 pm, we started our bedtime routine—brushing teeth, slipping into PJs, and picking out two stories to read. I pulled out my emotion cards next, and asked Jess how she was feeling. Jess was instantly curious. She picked "shy" and "scared"— "because it's a new place"—and also "happy" because "I met Sam and Dani and Peppa and Bron (our dogs)."

When it was time to climb into the top bunk, Jess suddenly froze. She panicked about how to get down, then started to cry, overwhelmed and frozen in fear. I reassured her gently and helped her down, offering the bottom bunk instead. But she was convinced it might fall on her. We switched the blankets, and I continued to reassure her calmly. Still, she couldn't settle. It was nearly midnight before she finally drifted off. I sat by her until I was sure she was asleep, then crept out and collapsed into bed.

Jess was up early the next morning—and so was I. We had Bluey on by 7 a.m. and were knee-deep in nail polish, cookie dough, and card games before lunchtime. We went to the beach, played outside, and took the dogs for a walk. She followed me everywhere, never comfortable being alone, constantly talking. She had little outbursts throughout the day—fake crying, yelling randomly, reacting to small things like a plastic spider, or touching warm water. But I didn't react to her yelling; I just continued on calmly, staying present and grounded.

She loved the dogs, though she occasionally used an angry tone with them or tried to put dirt on their fur. When I gently explained that muddy dogs couldn't come inside, she stopped immediately. She wasn't seeking attention from Sam as much as from me, but she loved it when we all played games together. She needed constant reassurance and often pushed boundaries to see how we'd respond. When she bumped her knee, thought she saw a worm, or made excuses not to go to bed, I needed to treat her like I would a much younger child—nurturing, calm, consistent.

The second night, when we did the emotion cards again, she picked "happy" and "strong".

"Because I found Sam's shoe, and he said I was a champion," she told me with pride. "So, I feel like a champion." It was so beautiful to see how one small word could bring so much encouragement to her.

Sunday rolled around, and it was time for Jess to go. As we

prepared to leave, her behaviours began again—yelling, short outbursts, restlessness. We didn't rush her. We took a few photos with the animals and kept reminding her of the plan: when we'd be leaving, where we were going, and who'd be there.

We met her caseworker at McDonald's. For the first time all weekend, Jess went quiet. When Sam and the caseworker went to order food, I sat with her in the booth.

Her eyes welled up. "Do I have to go?" she asked softly. "Can I stay with you?"

My heart cracked wide open. I pulled her in and gave her a big hug.

This little girl—who had once threatened a carer with violence, who'd experienced trauma most adults couldn't survive—just wanted to be loved. She wanted to belong somewhere.

"I wish you could, sweetheart," I whispered and pulled her closer.

I knew we couldn't keep her. I also knew she had no permanent placement waiting. Her previous placement had broken down. Her mother was in jail, her father in another state. She believed she'd go back to her mum when she was released—but everyone involved knew that was unlikely. She was in limbo, carrying the scars of a chaotic childhood marked by drug use, domestic violence and neglect.

Yet, in those two days, she sang pop songs with joy, painted her nails with care, played cards with a fierce competitiveness, and called herself a champion.

Maybe we'll see Jess again. Maybe we won't.

But I hope—and I truly believe—that for that one weekend, she felt safe. She felt loved. And maybe, just maybe, she'll carry a piece of that with her, wherever she ends up.

This respite was an intense but beautiful experience.

―――

OUR CONCERNS about the permanent match of the four children were increasing. It wasn't about our capacity to care for the children—we were ready. The real concern was whether we could continue to work with an agency that made decisions based on policies rather than the individual needs of the children and carers.

My emotions were so heightened, and I felt torn about how to move forward. One afternoon, I looked at Sam and said, "I need to get away."

He didn't hesitate. "Okay, let's do it."

Sam and I decided to step away for a couple of nights—to remove ourselves from the situation and have intentional time together to figure out what to do.

I booked accommodation a few hours away. The drive gave us space to breathe, talk, and process without the constant weight of the situation pressing in on us. We spent those two days turning everything over—what do we do? Could we make this work? Could we live with the alternative? We listed out the pros and cons, considering everything that had happened, how each of us felt, and what the consequences might be.

One thing was clear—we both had the same gut feeling: splitting these children up, even for six to twelve months, felt so wrong. And just as unsettling, we were losing our ability to trust the agency. Although Sam and I didn't see eye to eye on every detail, we agreed on the major points. Together, we decided to share our concerns with the caseworker.

We shared our fears with our caseworker, even mentioning that we might have to explore changing agencies if things didn't improve. That was the breaking point. The agency pulled the pin.

We never saw the children again.

THE LOSS WAS SHATTERING. What should have been one of the most joyful moments of our lives had turned into a nightmare. I had envisioned a future filled with laughter, milestones, and love. Now, my heart felt like it was breaking in slow motion, over and over again. The process had drained every ounce of joy and excitement from this journey, leaving only grief in its place.

Just a few months ago, I never imagined we'd be here. I had the next 15 years of my life planned out—a loving husband, a warm and comfortable home, and four beautiful children I loved with all my heart. Everything I had dreamed of, everything I had worked for, felt within reach. And then it all fell apart. Sam and I just cried. We had come to love these four kids so deeply.

We had built our lives around these children. Every decision, every plan, revolved around the belief that they would be with us forever.

Letting go and moving on has been agonising. We bought a van—a big 8-seater—just for them, to fit the sibling group we thought would be ours forever. After the match ended, Sam gently suggested we sell it and get something smaller, something more practical. We could use the money. But every time I thought about it, a wave of dread would rise up. Selling the van felt like giving up on the dream—on them.

Every day, as the weeks passed, I was reminded of the four children. Their room remained untouched for weeks before I could find the strength to pack it away. I put their stuffed animals in storage, threw out their toothbrushes, and wiped the slate clean—but their presence still lingered. The bug boxes we built together sat abandoned, the outdoor kitchen we made for them remained unused, and the silence in our house felt deafening.

One night, after a heated argument with Sam about the weight of everything we were going through, I retreated to our bedroom to cool off. My eyes landed on a plastic rose—the one the children had given me when I was sick during one of our weekends together. A lump formed in my throat as the weight of their absence crashed over me all over again. They were such wonderful kids. We had wanted to be their forever family. But the system—with all its complexities and constraints—ultimately stood in the way.

A few moments later, Sam walked in. He didn't say much at

first; he just sat beside me. Then he pulled me into his arms. "I'm sorry," he whispered.

"Me too," I said softly.

We didn't need to say anything more. The ache between us wasn't about the argument—it was about the loss. A loss too big for words.

We are not the type to give up easily. Sam, one of the most loyal and considerate people you'll ever meet, always puts others before himself. But even he saw it—we had fought as hard as we could, time and time again. And yet, no matter how much we gave, we had to accept that this wasn't our fight to win.

Those children will always hold a special place in our hearts, even though they are no longer in our lives.

TWO YEARS LATER, I still can't look at photos of them without tears welling up. I question everything. Did we make the wrong choices? Should we have bent to the agency's demands, no matter the cost, just to have them?

After the agency pulled the pin on the match of the four children, we told them we needed time to think about our next steps. We went back and forth, weighing the pros and cons, neither of us wanting to make a decision we'd later regret.

"I don't think we can trust the agency," Sam said, his voice heavy with frustration as he looked at me.

I nodded. "I agree." But doubt crept in as I considered the alternative. "I just worry that if we start with a new agency, we'll have to wait even longer. What if this agency finds us another match soon?"

"I get that," he said. "But can we really move forward with them when we don't trust them?"

I sighed, letting the question settle. Could we keep working with an agency that had let us down time and time again? Could we risk going through this all over again, hoping things would be different this time?

We took a few days to sit with it, running through every scenario, trying to balance logic with the emotional weight of it all. But in the end, the answer was clear.

We needed to change agencies. The trust had been broken too many times, and while our caseworker had been wonderful—one of the few bright spots in this experience—it wasn't enough. We were too weary, too drained to keep holding on to the hope that things would improve.

The more we thought about it, the more we realised we weren't alone in our frustration. We had heard story after story from other carers who had faced the same struggles with this agency. While I knew there were success stories out there, we couldn't ignore the pattern.

The agency asked us to stay. "You've really impressed the director," our caseworker mentioned casually one day after we'd provided respite care for a little boy. "And she's not someone who's easily impressed."

Although we were grateful for the compliment, it felt too risky to stay. It was time to move on.

Seeking guidance, we reached out to a friend at another agency. He assured us the decision was ours to make, but added that they would gladly welcome us if we wanted to shift to emergency and temporary care. It was comforting to know we had options, but the weight of the decision still loomed heavy.

My mentor, Ellen—someone who has walked the foster care journey for over 30 years and been a rock for me throughout ours—offered her perspective: we'd likely feel immense relief once we made the change. "It's not a life-altering decision," she said, though it certainly felt that way. The fear of stepping out of the familiar, no matter how broken it is, feels binding. I've faced so many tough battles in this journey, but the prospect of stepping into the unknown leaves me frozen. And yet, staying where we are isn't helping either. It's time to move forward, even if it feels like stepping off a cliff.

LOOKING BACK, I can see how naïve we were. We entered this world of foster care and adoption full of hope, believing that if we just did everything right, things would fall into place. But the reality was so much more complex. We didn't fully understand the system we were walking into—the layers of policies, the bureaucracy, the competing priorities of keeping families together while also ensuring children's safety and stability.

I don't want to place blame. I know there are people within the system who genuinely care, who are trying their best in an incredibly difficult space. But at the same time, I can't ignore the flaws we encountered—the miscommunications, the delays, the feeling of being strung along without real answers. If I could go back, I wouldn't just prepare myself for the emotional toll of fostering; I would prepare myself for the system itself. The waiting, the shifting timelines, and the way decisions sometimes felt like they were made with little regard for the children at the centre of it all.

We could have had a beautiful life with those kids, and I sometimes wonder what might have been if things had gone differently. But life is a series of choices, and we made ours with the best intentions and the information we had at the time. While the outcome was devastating, it was not without purpose. This experience shaped us, taught us hard but valuable lessons, and deepened our resolve to continue caring for children who need love and stability.

Though our forever family wasn't with those children, we've found beauty in our temporary care journey. We've built a life filled with purpose, one that carries the echoes of what we learned in those challenging days. And while the heartbreak will always be a part of me, so will the hope that those children are on their way to healing, just as we are.

Even through the heartbreak, even if I was only in their lives for a short time, I know that, for those moments, they were safe; they were loved, and they mattered.

Embracing Temporary

I never wanted to be a temporary carer. Not because there wasn't a need, but because I didn't think I could handle it. Plus, so many kids need forever homes, and I wanted to provide that stability to them. But we were in this position now where we couldn't move forward with the agency because of mistrust, and we weren't ready to go through the adoption process again with another agency, so we thought we'd go temporary for the time being and see if long-term kids come around later down the track.

We transitioned to the other agency as emergency carers. We had to transfer our documentation from the previous agency and then had a meeting with the new agency once that was complete. It took a couple of months for the transition to take place before being authorised. Within days of that finalising, we received a phone call from our new caseworker.

"We have an emergency; we need a crisis placement for these three children. Now, I can't tell you much about them except that they're of Aboriginal descent and classed as general foster care, which means they're normal."

"Normal? What does normal mean?" I thought.

I quickly moved on from that thought, as I was so excited about their arrival. I began to prepare the rooms, putting sheets on the beds and picking a stuffed animal for each bed. Oh, and I needed to do the shopping. My mind was running. Sam was out doing errands when they arrived, so I was on my own at home.

The caseworker's car pulled up. Two of the children, one boy and one girl, excitedly jumped out when they saw our large backyard with a cubby house. The third little one was asleep in her car seat. She woke up as the caseworker unbuckled her. They had three bags with smelly clothes and some blankets. I brought them inside and showed them around. They were loaded up with lots of energy and did not talk to me besides the occasional question while exploring their new environment.

The caseworker handed me the youngest child. "This is Siera, and that's Sean and Sally," she said, gesturing toward the older children.

"Thank you," I managed to say, but before I could ask anything more, she was already back in her car.

With a quick nod, she shut the door and drove off—no further explanation, no instructions, just gone.

I stood there, holding Siera in my arms, glancing at the older children who stared back at me with wary eyes. And just like that, they were mine to figure out.

―――

THEY SETTLED in well during those first few days. The transition seemed smooth at first. They went to sleep without fuss, explored our abundance of toys in the playroom and yard, and climbed on the play equipment. The eldest, Sean, six years old, was in primary school, while the two younger girls—Sally, just about four, and Siera, only sixteen months old—attended daycare two days a week.

Sam was working through it all, so most of the daily responsibilities fell to me—school drop-offs and pickups, meals, playtime, and navigating the emotional highs and lows of adjusting to new children. But he was hands-on where he could be, stepping in for bedtime routines, reading stories, and holding me up when I needed it.

Siera was already fiercely independent. She would push my hands away if I tried to help her with anything, determined to do things on her own, even when she clearly needed help. The middle child, Sally, had a sharpness to her—keen eyes always watching, quick to react, quick to demand. And the eldest, Sean, had a silence that spoke volumes.

He didn't say a word to anyone but me for days. At first, I thought he was just shy, adjusting. But a few days in, I had to run to the grocery store and mentioned offhandedly that I was about to leave. His face changed. Something about the way he looked at me, almost longingly, made me pause.

"Would you like to come with me?" I asked gently.

A big smile spread across his face as he nodded, eyes lighting up.

In the car, the quiet melted away. He talked my ear off the entire drive. Words tumbling out, excitement spilling over. As we walked into the shopping centre, he skipped beside me, chatting nonstop. I was taken aback—not because he was talking, but because he had been so silent before.

LATER, I learned from another school parent that Sean never spoke at school. Ever.

"What?" I asked, shocked.

"He just stares," the mother said. "Follows the other kids around, but never says a word."

His teacher confirmed it. Told me he would just stand by a pole in the middle of the playground, watching silently.

I was stunned. At home now, he never stopped talking. It hit me then—he felt safe with us.

FAMILY CONTACT WAS RELENTLESS. Because of different fathers, Siera had five visits a week, Sally two or three, and Sean one or two, depending on whether his grandparents were involved. It was exhausting—not only emotionally for the children and for us, but also a constant logistical nightmare to manage.

For the kids, it was an emotional rollercoaster—seeing their birth family, then having to return and try to settle again. For us, it meant endless practical demands: organising drop-offs and pick-ups, coordinating with different workers and caseworkers, and constantly reshuffling our days around contact schedules. We never had the chance to find a steady rhythm at home. Just as we'd start to settle, the routine was disrupted again, leaving the children unsettled and often re-triggered, and us scrambling to hold things together.

Siera—just sixteen months—was being pulled in so many directions, and I could see the toll it was taking. She had no real attachment to anyone. She would lift her hands to be picked up by anyone, strangers included. It made my heart ache.

She mostly slept on her own. When I put her down, she would go straight to sleep without asking for cuddles, pats, or any comfort. One of the first nights, when it was time for bedtime, I tried to rock her and soothe her like you can imagine you would. But it felt like such gestures were foreign to her.

One evening, after trying to rub her back, which only disturbed her more, I walked out and shut the door. I didn't know what to do. Should I continue doing what she was used to —just putting her down and leaving? Or should I try to bond with her by showing affection through cuddles at bedtime? Would that even help her development and attachment, or was I setting myself up for failure and sleepless nights?

I was full of questions, but didn't know who to ask. This wasn't your typical first-time mum situation.

THERE WAS A MOMENT, about six weeks in, when I thought we were making progress. She seemed like she wanted my comfort more. She relaxed into my arms as I held her before bed. I felt some relief that maybe this was improving. But just as quickly as the thought arrived, it faded. The next day, she was as distant as ever.

I had always assumed bonding with a baby would be simple. Meet their basic needs—food, sleep, cuddles, play—and the connection would follow. With most babies, it does. But this child wasn't that baby. Instead of melting into my arms, she stiffened. Instead of seeking comfort, she turned away. I expected her to eventually relax into me the way babies are "supposed" to, but she never did. The very idea of parental comfort seemed foreign to her.

Building bonds with the others was more difficult than I expected as well. Sally was the same at bedtime. We tried sitting with her until she fell asleep—offering comfort—but she wouldn't stay still, instead giving attitude or whining endlessly. Eventually, leaving her in bed seemed like the best option. This wasn't at all what I was expecting. I was expecting children who were desperate for an adult's affection. But these children didn't seem like they wanted any. They didn't even cry for their birth parents, which I found odd.

ONE EVENING, Sally's screams pierced the silence of the night, jolting me awake. My heart pounded as I rushed into her room, finding her thrashing and wailing, eyes squeezed shut in terror. Panicked, I scooped her up, whispering soft reassurances as I carried her out to the lounge room, desperate not to wake her siblings.

Sam was already there, waiting to support. Together, we tried everything—rocking her, holding her close, speaking in soothing tones. Nothing worked. She screamed as if she were trapped in a nightmare she couldn't escape. I cradled her, rubbing her back, but she remained inconsolable. Defeated, I passed her to Sam, hoping a different touch might help.

We sat there for what felt like an eternity, helpless and unsure of what to do. And then, just as suddenly as it began, it stopped. Her body relaxed, her breathing steadied, and she slumped against Sam's chest in exhaustion.

Without a word, we carried her back to bed, tucking her in as if the past few hours hadn't happened. But as we stood in the doorway, watching her sleep peacefully, we were left with no more clarity than we had at the start. No idea what had triggered it. No idea what, if anything, had soothed her. Only the lingering unease that it would happen again.

THEN, as the weeks went on, it got harder. The sleepless nights felt endless, and I knew—on a rational level—that this was to be expected. These kids had been through so much, and I understood that settling into a new home would be messy. But knowing it was "normal" didn't make it any easier to live through.

It wasn't just the sleepless nights. It was the defiant behaviours, the constant sibling fighting, the uneaten meals, and my own insecurities and grief bubbling to the surface. I felt overwhelmed and ashamed. I had spent so much time preparing for this, reading the books, taking the training, and telling myself I was ready. So, why wasn't I coping better? Why couldn't I shake the feeling that I wasn't cut out for this?

At that moment, I felt like I was failing. I couldn't reconcile my knowledge of what I "should" expect with the weight of what I was actually feeling. It was more than exhaustion; it was the sinking realisation that my expectations were unrealistic. I had gone into this thinking I could handle anything. I had done so well with the first large sibling group, but the reality of parenting *these* children was testing me in ways I hadn't imagined.

Nothing about these kids was what I expected.

Building bonds with them was far from easy. We tried everything, but nothing "normal" or taught in training seemed to work. Those first few months were painful. I was a new mum to three children, and I felt utterly unqualified for the job.

Looking back now, I see how normal my struggles were and how many other carers have likely sat in the same place, wondering if they were good enough. If I could speak to that version of myself, I'd tell her it's okay to feel this way—that those feelings don't make her less of a carer. But at that moment, all I could feel was the weight of my perceived failures.

OUR CASEWORKER VISITED for a check-up a couple of months in. She asked how I was doing.

"I'm not sure I can continue to do this," I said in an exhausted tone.

She didn't show much sympathy, but simply responded that I was just tired, and we'd figure it out. She was right, but it didn't offer me any relief. Honestly, there probably wasn't much more she could say. She was right. I was just tired. The messiness of this was to be expected.

The next day, I was so overwhelmed by the past couple of months that I sat in our pantry, bawling my eyes out, so unsure of what to do or how to get through this. "I'm not cut out for these kids," I thought to myself.

As the days and weeks continued to pass, I struggled. I didn't feel the love for these kids that I thought I'd have. They were so difficult and defiant, and their temperaments were completely opposite to mine. I thought back to our match for adoption and couldn't help but feel a mix of grief and frustration. *These weren't the ones I wanted. I wanted my first ones, the ones I loved.*

My hope was crushed because we had believed so much in our forever sibling group match, and that didn't pan out. I was so excited about those four kids. I sat on the end of my bed one morning as those feelings flowed through me and silently reminded myself, "There is no going back. The four children are gone, no longer an option for us, and are split up between two different families now. That is huge, and this is hard, but we'll get through this." I wiped my tears and went back and attended to the children.

I kept searching for answers—someone to tell me what was wrong with these kids, with me, and what to do. I didn't realise it then, but I was learning too. Each hard moment taught me something about them, about myself. I was not only learning their triggers and fears, but I was also learning my own and how to parent through them.

CHRISTMAS WAS APPROACHING, and with it, a long-awaited holiday. The past four months had been a relentless cycle of struggles, exhaustion pressing in from all sides. I had spent too many moments hiding in the pantry, wiping away tears of frustration, and wondering if we would ever truly connect. But something shifted during those two weeks away.

Within the first 24 hours, Sally fell sick—not just a mild cold, but a deep, relentless cough that rattled through her tiny frame. Her small body shuddered with each breath, and for the first time, she allowed herself to lean into me for comfort. That night, as I lay beside her, rubbing her back between coughing fits, I felt a quiet gratitude. She sought me out. She let me be the one to soothe her.

Sam, seeing my exhaustion, gently offered, "Why don't you go sleep in the spare room? I can stay with her."

I shook my head. "No, I'm good," I whispered, unwilling to move. Yes, I was tired—drained, even—but I wasn't going to miss this chance to bond with her. After all the walls she had put up, this moment of closeness felt too important to step away from.

During the day, her stubbornness remained as strong as ever. She refused to nap, no matter how unwell she felt. But instead of battling her, I adjusted. While Siera slept and Sean played, I took Sally for midday walks—just the two of us.

As we wandered through the open grass plains, she was quiet, lost in her own world. Then, in a single unthinking moment, she reached for my hand.

I exhaled, a warmth spreading through me. Maybe—just maybe—we were getting somewhere.

By the end of the holiday, I had a renewed sense of joy, realising how grateful I was to have these children to love.

As we came back home, back into routine, the familiar difficulties began to surface again. We poured so much effort into settling the children and creating a stable routine, but the constant disruption of frequent family contact made it an uphill battle. The kids were often dysregulated and emotionally unsettled, leaving us struggling to rebuild their sense of security. Each visit brought a different agency worker—usually someone they had never met before—and the impact was obvious. These weren't trusted faces; they were strangers.

I thought especially of Siera, still so little. Her fragile attachment was being chipped away day by day by the revolving door of unfamiliar people in her life. "How is this okay?" I wondered.

BEFORE I GO ANY FURTHER, I want to be clear: I am not against birth families or their right to see their children. These are their kids, after all. However, I am a firm believer in prioritising the well-being of the child, no matter the situation. From my experience—and from the experiences of the countless other foster carers I've spoken to—it often feels as though the rights of the parents are placed above the needs of the child. That imbalance can have devastating consequences.

EVEN THOUGH OUR bonding was difficult and attachment issues were evident, it was improving, and for that, I was so grateful.

One evening, we had friends over for dinner. It was late, and the two eldest had already gone to bed, but Siera just wouldn't settle. Finally, we brought her out of her room to sit with us at the table.

She looked at the unfamiliar faces around her, studying them for a moment before flashing a small, trusting smile. Then, without hesitation, she nestled into my chest. I felt her little body relax against mine, and at that moment, I realised—maybe we were making a difference. Maybe, despite all the challenges, she was beginning to see us as home.

Warmth spread through me as she snuggled closer. Then, after a moment, she turned and reached for Sam, settling against him just as easily. I caught his eye, and we shared a quiet understanding—this was progress. With all the disruptions she had endured, all the broken attachments, there was still hope.

She was learning to trust. And maybe, just maybe, we were becoming her safe place.

PARENTHOOD WAS nothing like I had imagined. Early on, I found myself not enjoying it at all. *It's not supposed to be this way,* I thought over and over again. Desperate for guidance, I devoured every book I could find, searching for answers and reassurance.

One day, I came upon the book *Post Adoption Blues,* which became a lifeline. It confronted the shame I felt and validated the emotions I was too afraid to voice. It shared stories of other carers who struggled to enjoy parenting an adoptive or foster child, normalising the challenges and affirming that it's okay not to love every moment.

One story, in particular, stood out as I read it. A young mother had adopted a 3-year-old, believing she would thrive as a full-time stay-at-home parent. But things didn't go as planned. Overwhelmed and struggling, she sought professional advice. The recommendation was simple but profound: send the child to daycare and return to work. That decision saved their relationship, and over time, things improved.

Her story mirrored mine. I thought I would want to be home full-time with the children, but it didn't work out the way I had hoped. I needed more help. I contacted the caseworker, desperate for more daycare for the younger children. She agreed to help and began the search, thankfully finding a couple more days for them.

I know daycare isn't ideal in every way. But for me, it was a lifesaver at the time. It gave me the sanity to return home and be the parent they needed me to be. Those few days of respite allowed me to recharge and show up fully for them. My heart would break when they cried as I dropped them off, but I remind myself often that taking care of my well-being is essential for their well-being, too. I couldn't meet their needs if I didn't give myself a chance to recover.

WE FINALLY STARTED FINDING a groove with these kids. It wasn't perfect, but we were beginning to mesh. Slowly, the chaos settled into something resembling a rhythm. One day, the caseworker called to check in.

"It's going really well," I told her. "Everything feels smooth."

She sounded pleased and went on to explain that it didn't look like the children would be able to return to their family. Then, she asked the question that filled us with hope: Would we consider long-term care for them?

The progress we had made with the children felt like a hard-earned victory, and the thought of them staying with us long-term brought us so much joy. We both agreed that we would be very happy to have the children stay long-term and told the caseworker.

BUT JUST AS QUICKLY AS the possibility of long-term care arrived, it vanished. The agency informed us a few weeks later that the children would be moving to live with a distant relative named Maria within a couple of months.

It was devastating. How quickly things changed. This time, we were more prepared for the heartbreak, though. At the time of the news, we were in the process of moving to a new house, so we told the agency it would be best for the children to transition to their new placement before our move.

We dropped them off at their grandparents' house, where they would stay temporarily until Maria was ready to take them. Saying goodbye was every bit as hard as we expected. The youngest two were oblivious to what was really happening when we dropped them off. Sean reached out to us as we walked away from the porch. We waved goodbye. "Love you, sweetheart," I called out. It was a sad time without them in our care, but travel, moving house, and jobs kept us busy and distracted from the heartache.

THREE MONTHS PASSED. We moved into our new home, started new jobs, and waited for a new placement. Then, one day, while I was completing my induction at my new job, my phone buzzed with a familiar name on the screen.

The children's caseworker.

"Weird," I thought as I stepped out to answer the call.

She greeted me politely, asked how I was, and then quickly got to the point. "Would you consider having the children return to your care? There have been some significant doubts about their placement with Maria, and we're wondering if you'd take them back for the time being."

I was stunned—and thrilled. The thought of seeing them again filled me with excitement. *Maybe this time, they'll stay forever,* I thought, only to quickly push that hope aside, reminded of the unpredictability of foster care.

A couple of weeks later, I hopped on a flight to bring them back. My heart was racing with nerves. *How will they respond? Will they want to come back?* The caseworker reassured me over the phone that they still spoke of us often during her visits.

I waited anxiously outside the departure area as the caseworker arrived with the kids.

Sean came first. He was quiet and shy, but he hugged me—not unusual for him. Once the workers left, he relaxed and returned to his normal self, his excitement bubbling over.

A few months later, as we sat on his bed during our bedtime routine, he looked up at me and said, "You know, when I saw you at the airport, I was really excited to see you."

I pulled him close. "I know, sweetheart. And I was so excited to see you, too."

Back at the airport, I waited with Sean—then Sally and Siera arrived. "Mummy! Mummy! Mummy!" they screamed as they jumped out of the car and ran toward me.

Oh, my heart melted. My babies. I wrapped them in my arms, holding on tightly.

We flew back together, their chatter and laughter filling the plane, and we returned to our new home as a family once more.

―――

WE KNEW the children had a younger brother, Scotty, who was in care with another foster carer. Months earlier, we had expressed interest in taking him on, but his current carer wanted to keep him until there was more certainty about the case.

Then, one day, a couple of weeks after the three children had returned, the caseworker asked, "Would you take their little brother also?"

"Yes, of course. Four children aren't that much different than three," I replied confidently. I laugh now when I think back on that comment—how naïve I was!

A month later, I had a flight booked to pick up Scotty. We were so excited to finally have all four siblings together under one roof. It felt like we were completing a puzzle, bringing the missing piece home.

It's true—every child is unique. With every child who has come into our home, we've had to learn how to parent and connect with them in their own way. By this point, I had grown to love the three children deeply. The challenges we had faced together had bonded us in ways I never expected. But when Scotty arrived, something shifted. He brought something entirely different to our family. He shifted something in me.

I'm not sure exactly why he had such an impact on my heart. Perhaps it was because he was the youngest child we had ever cared for, or maybe it was the way he adored me so completely. His affection melted my heart in ways I hadn't anticipated. For the first time, I felt what it was like to be truly needed in a way that felt pure and unconditional. Our attachment felt easy; he melted completely into my arms with complete trust.

Having the six of us together—keeping the siblings united—felt like a small victory amid a system that often struggles to keep siblings together.

Becoming Parents

It was amazing and beautiful to have the siblings together, and we thought the fact that they were all with us meant maybe we would be able to keep the siblings together with us forever. It was exciting, but also super challenging. We were learning how to be parents to four little people, and it wasn't easy.

We didn't have the typical progression into parenthood. We went from being childless to caring for four children—aged 12 months to 6 years—in what felt like the blink of an eye. Beyond the sheer number of little ones, we had to learn how to be parents while also navigating the complexities of caring for children who had experienced trauma.

MOTHER'S DAY ROLLED AROUND, and it felt weird. I played the role of mum to the kids in my care, but they also didn't always call me mum. At times, when they were sad or upset, they'd cry for Mummy, which was me. Or when I'd pick them up from daycare, they would occasionally say "Mum!" and run to me. It was beautiful, and it filled my heart with affection, but it didn't feel natural. One of the foster care agencies taught us about "tummy mummies" and "everyday mummies", which made sense.

It was a simple way to explain that they had two mummies. So, we went with it.

With it being Mother's Day, the topic came up, and I continued to tell them they had two mummies and two daddies who loved them very much. It seemed to help them and, I guess, helped me, too. I was being their mum. No, I didn't birth them, but I'm still their mum, even though I didn't always feel like it.

IT'S ALWAYS a bit awkward explaining who you are to people when you have foster kids. Daycare workers often ask, "What do they call you?" And then there are moments like at school pickup, when a teacher hesitates mid-sentence, saying "Here's your... er... What does she call you?"

I was called many names. Sometimes it was my first name, sometimes a nickname, and sometimes "Mum." It depended on the moment. But when it really mattered, I knew I was their safe place.

If I'm honest, I wanted them to call me Mum. I thought it might make me feel more like a mother. One day, I overheard Siera—three years old at the time—call out to my friend, whose own child calls her Mum: *"Mum! Can I do colouring?"* My chest tightened, and my heart sank. She had so casually given that name to someone else when it had taken her so long to give it to me. I knew she was just copying her friend, innocent in the moment, but it still stung.

I reminded myself that they shouldn't call me Mum unless they truly wanted to, and I would never force it. Still, deep down, I longed for it. I knew I wasn't the mum they wanted. They wanted their birth mum—and understandably so.

BECOMING a mum takes a kind of growing up, a reshaping of yourself. But becoming "Mum" to children who long for someone else requires a different kind of maturity altogether. It's holding the role with open hands, loving fully while knowing you may never be the one they truly wish for.

At times, I've felt guilty for wanting them to call me Mum. It's as if I'm supposed to say I don't care—but I do care. And that's not wrong. Of course, the burden should never be placed on the child, and I would never demand it, but denying my own longing for recognition doesn't make it go away. We carry the daily responsibility of caring for these children, and being seen in that role matters. We're not replacing their birth parents, but what we do matters too.

So I want to speak directly to the foster mum—or dad—who is aching to hear that word. I know how deeply you want them to call you Mum. I did, too. And it's okay to want that. It's not about ego; it's about identity. It's about longing to be seen for the role you live out day after day.

But here's what I've learned: even if they never say the word, you are still showing up as their mum. Your presence. Your patience. Your gentle voice and open arms. These are the things they will carry with them. "Mum" is just a word—the safety they feel with you is what will leave the deepest imprint on their hearts.

One afternoon, I came home from work and Sean, now 7 years old, had written me a note, "Your My best Mum in the holl intia planet" (You're the best mum in the whole entire planet), with two stick figures holding hands. Tears filled my eyes. "Man, this job is hard," I thought. "But so worth it."

There was an upcoming family gathering, so we were asked to take a trip to see the kids' birth family. The whole family was there for a gathering. We were told by the agency to just drop them off and go. So that's what we did. Initially, the kids were okay. Excited to see their birth family.

As we began to leave, they began to cry and reach for us, but we continued to wave goodbye. There was nothing we could do, so we drove off. We returned a couple hours later to pick them up, and they yelled and ran to us. I pulled them in tight.

Sally looked at me and said, "Don't you ever leave me with these people again," with tears streaming down her face. My heart broke. These people were part of her birth family, but there was a clear disconnect—she didn't feel safe with them the way she did with us.

Some might say it was our fault—that Sally lacked connection with her family because we didn't do enough. But the truth is, Sally had lived with them for three years before coming to us. Her early years were spent with her birth family, including her mother, and even while in our care she had regular contact with them. She had every opportunity to build and maintain that cultural and familial connection. Yet despite all that, it was clear she didn't feel emotionally safe with them. She felt safe with us. We were her home, her everyday comfort.

And still, we were told to just drop her off and walk away, leaving her with people she barely knew how to trust. We would have gladly stayed—with open arms and open hearts—to support her through it. But because we were "just foster carers," our presence wasn't considered important.

I'm not in the business of keeping children from their families. But when a child responds like Sally did, I can't help but question the benefit of prioritising biology and culture over a child's lived experience of safety and belonging. In foster care, the system so often defaults to blood ties—yet what matters most for children is not biology, but the humans who make them feel secure.

A few weeks later, as we sat and read our bedtime stories, Sally picked *Little Miss Spider*. The last line is my favourite: "For finding your mother, there's one certain test. You must look for the creature who loves you the best." As I read that line, she snuggled in closer. In that quiet moment, I was reminded of the love and safety she found in me.

———

BECOMING a mother revealed my triggers more and more—the ones I thought I'd dealt with, but that became glaringly obvious in the heat of parenting. Parenting triggered more than just frustration—it tapped into deeper hurts. I pour so much love into my children. I play with them, offer consistent affection, and respond to their attention-seeking behaviour with patience. I try to move slowly and gently, hoping my efforts will resonate with them. Sometimes, they do. But other times, their defiance feels like a slap in the face. It's not just about the one moment—it's the accumulation of all the moments leading up to it. It feels wrong to be so angry at a child, and yet, it's there. I feel shame at the feelings I have.

The anger and defiance of Siera, in particular, could trigger me almost instantly. I came to realise that while "time-ins" were ideal in theory, they weren't always possible in moments when I was emotionally overwhelmed. I never wanted to act out of anger, so I learned that sometimes the best thing I could do—for both of us—was to create a safe bit of space. My mentor, Ellen, once told me, "Sometimes you just need to put them in a time-out. The caseworker might not like it, but you've got to do what helps you stay calm."

At first, that advice felt wrong to me. I had clung tightly to the idea that I'd always follow what we learned in the foster care training. But parenting children with trauma brings layers of complexity. One afternoon, after trying everything to soothe a screaming toddler, I walked Siera to her cot, put her down, closed the door, and stepped away. I watched her on the baby monitor, her screams echoing through the room, the dummy flying across the space. I sat on the edge of my bed, head in hands, asking myself, "How do I do this?"

I took a few deep breaths and returned to Siera a moment

later. I picked her up, gave her a hug, and brought her back to the playroom. We embraced briefly before she moved on, happily distracted by her toys. It wasn't perfect, but it was real. I didn't walk away out of anger—I walked away because I love her and needed a moment to reset so I could show up for her again, the way she deserved.

People are often critical of time-outs, but sometimes, you just need a moment to breathe. The kids are safe in their beds, and I only step away just long enough to regulate myself. Then I return, grounded and ready to offer comfort. It's not about punishment; it's about protecting the connection and making sure I can show up as the calm, safe adult they need.

Years later, while holding another young child during a check-up, the nurse gently said, *"Sometimes babies just cry. It's okay to put them down in their cot—they're safe there—and go make yourself a cup of tea."*

Relieved, I responded, *"Thank you for that advice."* I only wished someone had told me that when I first began parenting. All the trauma-informed and foster care training had drilled into me that I must always do time-ins, that leaving a child alone could cause harm. I wish someone had also told me it was okay to step away for a moment—that sometimes, walking away is part of being a good parent too.

———

AS OTHER PARENTS CAN APPRECIATE, the journey into parenthood highlights some of our deep triggers and hurts. Along with the normal challenges of parenthood, we also had added pressures that come along with foster care as well.

Discipline is one of the greatest challenges in foster care. Every parent faces moments of frustration, questioning their own approach—am I being too harsh? Too lenient? What actually works? But in foster care, the stakes feel higher. Every misstep feels scrutinised. The weight of getting it wrong can be overwhelming.

I wanted to be the perfect carer—the one who always

responded with patience, who never raised her voice, and who always followed the trauma-informed approaches we were taught. But real life isn't a training manual. When exhaustion takes over, when every strategy seems to fail, when the behaviours escalate despite my best efforts, doubt creeps in. Am I failing them? Am I a bad carer?

ONE AFTERNOON, I sat in my office at work, hands clenched, listening to caseworkers discuss reports on carers who lost their patience. The caseworkers judged the carer for her actions and proceeded to write the required reports. Inside, I knew they needed to do this, but as a current carer who has not always responded positively to my children, fear arose inside me.

I've seen the fear in other carers' eyes when they confess, "I yelled today," wondering if a moment of frustration will define them. Parents outside the system don't live with this same level of scrutiny. They don't have to second-guess whether their natural instincts to set firm boundaries or enforce consequences might be misinterpreted as something harmful.

What do you do when nothing seems to work? When the defiance escalates, when every consequence feels ineffective, when the same behaviour repeats despite every positive reinforcement and trauma informed strategy in the book? It's easy to feel powerless. I found myself questioning, "What now?"

More than once, I sat on the kitchen floor, tears streaming down my face, feeling utterly lost. I didn't want to yell. I didn't want to feel this way. But the fear weighed on me. The guilt of losing patience. The pressure of always needing to do better. And the unspoken worry that if I got it wrong, these children—children I had come to love—could be taken from me.

"I lost it with the kids today," I sheepishly said to Sam as he arrived home from work.

"I shouldn't have yelled," I added, my voice quieter now. "But I had just had enough."

"That's okay." He pulled me in. "Don't be so hard on yourself, babe." I'm so grateful for a partner who didn't judge me when I messed up.

If you're a carer struggling with challenging behaviours and discipline, you're not alone. It's okay to admit when it's hard. It's okay to ask for help. You don't have to carry the shame of imperfection in silence. None of us has all the answers. What matters is that we keep showing up, keep learning, and keep striving to do better—for them and ourselves.

NORMAL PARENTS often follow a concept known as "good enough parenting," which essentially means that as long as you're doing a good job about half of the time, that's sufficient. Research shows that parenting well half of the time is usually enough for a child to turn out okay. However, this standard doesn't apply to foster parents. Foster parents are held to an expectation of perfection—no mistakes allowed. If mistakes happen, they risk being reprimanded or even losing their ability to foster.

It's an enormous burden to carry: the expectation of perfection. Not only are you navigating the challenges of parenting in general and the unique challenges of parenting someone else's child, but you're also expected to do it flawlessly.

This expectation just breeds shame and secrecy. There is a shame surrounding foster carers and their inability to share their mistakes. Even with other carers, you end up speaking in code, knowing they understand, but also never speaking the words of your failures because that could be used against you. I'm so grateful I had another carer in my life who spoke that code and didn't judge me for my mistakes. She empathised with my struggles and offered support.

Even as I write this book, I find myself wondering, *"Will people misunderstand what I've shared? Will I be reprimanded? Will agency workers judge me for not being a perfect parent—and could that jeopardise my ability to continue fostering?"*

So why share your mistakes? You might ask. Because I believe that if we want to gain more foster carers, retain the ones we have, and ultimately see more children in loving homes, we need to be more honest about the reality of this work. Carers can't be expected to be perfect. That expectation is not only unrealistic—it's harmful. We need to start pulling down that pressure by speaking more openly, supporting each other in our shortcomings, and creating a culture where honesty is met with grace, not judgment.

The line often feels so blurry. Yelling at a child in frustration isn't the same as abuse—yet in foster care, it can be treated that way. All parents lose their cool at times, but as carers, every raised voice, every imperfect moment, feels magnified under scrutiny. An accusation for something so human felt deeply unfair, and it left me constantly second-guessing myself, wondering if I was allowed to parent like a real mum at all.

I've come to see that many people do understand parenting is hard and that foster carers can't be perfect. But not everyone. There will always be some workers who judge harshly, which is why it's important to be discerning about who you open up to. The expectation that carers must parent flawlessly is unfair and unrealistic. If you find yourself struggling or falling short, know this—you are not alone, and the pressure for perfection is unjust.

THE FEAR of accusations haunted me. I was terrified that one day, a child might tell a worker that I had yelled at them, and just like that, all the children would be taken away. I had seen other mothers raise their voices at their kids in frustration, without a second thought, without fear of losing everything. Meanwhile, I lay awake at night, replaying every tough moment, wondering if one sentence could strip me of everything I had fought for.

One afternoon, the phone rang. My stomach clenched. Calls from the caseworker were always unpredictable—sometimes good, sometimes bad, but never insignificant. I hesitated before answering, inhaling sharply.

"Dani, I hate to do this, but I have to bring something to your attention." The caseworker's voice was gentle but firm. "You've been reported."

My breath caught. Reported? My mind whirled, grasping for answers. What could it be?

"One of the workers who visited your home the other day reported some concerns," she continued carefully. "The lock on your medical cabinet was unlocked when she was there last. The bathwater was still in the tub. And Scotty's cot—it's too high. It needs to be lowered."

My stomach dropped. That was it? That was why I was having this conversation?

I exhaled, forcing my voice to stay steady. "The lock was unlocked, yes, but it was still there. We were rushing that morning and just didn't relock it. And the bathwater? Yeah, I guess I forgot to unplug it in the rush. And Scotty—we watch him like a hawk. He's never once tried to climb out of the cot. I know him. He won't try."

The caseworker sighed, her sympathy evident. "I get it. I've probably left bathwater in the tub before with my own kids." There was a pause before she added, "But I still have to report it. It's procedure."

Procedure. That word again.

I nodded, even though she couldn't see me. "Understood. I'll relock the cabinet. I'll make sure to unplug the bath water. I'll lower the cot. Whatever needs to be done."

She thanked me, apologetic but firm, and the call ended.

I turned to Sam, who had been listening from the kitchen. His jaw was tight, hands clenched into fists at his sides.

"It's so invasive," he spat, his voice thick with anger. "I feel violated. They come into our home, into our lives, and do that? It's so unfair."

I reached for his hand, but he pulled away, pacing. "I want to call the caseworker," he said, his voice low, controlled—but simmering with frustration.

"Will it change anything?" I asked softly.

"I don't care. She needs to know how unfair this is."

He grabbed his phone and dialled. I watched as he explained, his voice taut but measured. To my surprise, she listened. She didn't dismiss him, didn't push back.

"I get it," she said. "I really do. And I appreciate you sharing how you feel."

When he hung up, he exhaled heavily, rubbing his hands over his face. "I know it doesn't fix anything, but at least I said something."

I nodded.

But even as we moved on with our day, the weight of it lingered—the knowledge that no matter how well we cared for these kids, we would always be watched. Scrutinised. Judged. And one small misstep—one unlocked cabinet, one forgotten bath—could make it all come crashing down.

OVER TIME, things did get easier. The fear of accusations never completely disappeared, but I learned to focus on what I could control—loving the kids as best I could and letting go of the rest.

Still, the anxiety had a way of creeping back in. Parenting is demanding, and no one can stay calm every moment of every day. It's normal to lose your cool sometimes—to raise your voice or snap in frustration. Yet whenever it happened, I felt like it wasn't okay for me.

ONE AFTERNOON, after a particularly hard moment with the kids, I picked up the phone and called Ellen. I couldn't shake the fear that I'd done something wrong.

"Those moments happen," Ellen said gently. "And they will

happen to you. But listen—you are doing an amazing job. I've seen you with those kids. They are so loved. Sometimes, you just have to go through it. The last worker who hit me with a false accusation told me outright—they knew it wasn't true, but they still had to go through the process. It's just protocol. The workers know you. They see you with the kids. Your character will shine through, beautiful."

Ellen's words steadied me. It was the unfortunate reality of fostering—accusations happen. Carers often say, *"It's not if you get an accusation, it's when."* Agencies have to take every report seriously, and I understood why. Children in care *do* get abused, and real accusations *do* get dismissed too easily.

But that's what made it such a hard space to exist in. Some children, shaped by past trauma, will say things that weren't true—sometimes as a test, sometimes as a defence mechanism, sometimes without fully understanding the consequences. Most workers knew this. They didn't blindly believe every word a child said, but they still had to follow procedures.

It was a delicate, exhausting balance. I just had to trust that my love, my actions, and my character would speak louder than fear.

———

WE'VE HAD to find our own way. I read all the parenting books, searching for answers. The advice was helpful, but in the end, I realised we needed to figure out what worked for *us* and the specific children in our care. Timeouts in bedrooms worked for some but were disastrous for others. A hug on the couch soothed some children, while others needed their space—and sometimes, I needed space, too. There were moments when the only option was to walk away, take a deep breath, and try again later.

Parenting books offer countless strategies, but no single method works for every family or every child. It's all trial and error. I've made mistakes—every parent and carer has. Expecting perfection from ourselves is neither fair nor realistic. What matters is how we respond to those mistakes. We apologise. We model humility. And above all, we show a lot of love.

The majority of people just don't understand that it is so different parenting your own children compared to foster children. The complexities that come along with foster care add so much to the parenting role that biological parents just can't comprehend. Much like a person without a child can't fully understand the challenges of someone with a child.

ONE EVENING, I spoke with a friend on the phone; she began to mention her kids and what was going on, and I could hear them in the background. She asked about the foster kids we had, and I shared a brief update on how they were. At this time, we were going through a challenging time bonding with the children, and each day seemed like a struggle.

As I shared about our children, the lack of commonality hit me. "The challenges I'm facing are nothing like hers. She's got children of her own who are biologically connected to her. She's had them since before they were born. They know her, and she knows them. There is no question about their connection. Whereas mine is new, uneasy, and lacking," the thoughts raced as I tried to listen to her response.

IN SO MANY WAYS, parenting these kids is different. It's not just providing love and care; you have to navigate the layers of trauma, attachment challenges, birth family dynamics, and the constant pressure of being a perfect foster parent.

Parenting these kids has been nothing like I imagined. The trials have pushed me to my limits, forced me to confront parts of myself I didn't know existed, and challenged every expectation I had about what being a parent should look like. It's not always easy to admit that I don't enjoy every moment of this journey or that I've struggled to feel like a "real" mum. But I've learned that being a parent isn't about perfection or biology—it's about showing up, day after day, even when it's hard.

Every tear, every hug, and every bedtime story has taught me something about resilience, love, and the healing power of presence. Sitting with my kids one lazy afternoon, I realised they didn't care about my flaws or my doubts. They didn't need me to be perfect—they just wanted me to be there. In that moment, I understood that sometimes love is as simple as being present, even in the messiness of life.

We're still learning to be their parents, and they're still learning to trust us as their safe place. The path hasn't been easy, but it's in these small, quiet moments of connection that I'm reminded why this journey is worth it. Being a foster parent isn't about achieving an ideal; it's about offering love and stability in a world that has often denied them both. And for now, being enough is more than enough.

Uncertainty & Working in the System

Living in uncertainty is one of the hardest parts of fostering—your heart is torn apart over and over again. For more than two years, this case teetered on the edge, swinging unpredictably between permanence and separation. One day, it seemed certain the children would stay with us forever; the next, it felt like their departure was inevitable. The constant back-and-forth was emotionally draining, each shift reopening wounds that had barely begun to heal.

Sam and I are usually resilient and able to put on a strong front, even when things feel overwhelming. But one afternoon, as we sat on the couch in exhausted silence, he finally admitted, "I think this is taking more of a toll on me than I realised. The uncertainty... It's just so hard."

I exhaled, nodding. "Yeah, I agree."

Neither of us said anything more. We just sat there, the weight of the unknown pressing down on us, heavy and suffocating—because no matter how much we wanted clarity, no matter how deeply we loved these kids, the decision was never ours to make.

As the agency worked to determine the children's long-term placement, they asked us to take them to visit Maria so they could assess her suitability for permanent care of them. We agreed. After a long flight with four children, we arrived in a small rural town at a simple motel for our few-night stay. The next day, we drove to Maria's home to drop off the children. It was a small, simple two-bedroom cottage with sheets blocking the light from entering the room. The assessor was present when we arrived, and we did the general niceties. The TV was on, and the kids soon began watching. While distracted, we left.

My heart ached as I dropped the children off with Maria. It was only for a few hours, but it felt so much heavier than that. This was the person who might take them forever. She was the children's biological family, and she was of the same cultural background. She was always kind to us, but I questioned her capability to care for four young children with complex needs. I didn't want to keep the kids away from her, but I also wanted what was best for the children. *"Will it be the best?"* I couldn't help but wonder.

We picked the children up two hours later, and they were watching a movie. "Did they watch TV the whole time?" I wondered. "How will the assessor get any kind of evidence of her capacity if they're just watching TV?"

I hoped that this would be reflected in the assessment, but I'm not so sure it was.

After the trip, we felt more certain—there was no way that Maria would be approved to care for all four children. She simply didn't have the capacity. Wanting to ensure the agency had a full picture of the situation, we sent an email outlining our observations—not to criticise her, but to provide an honest assessment of her ability to manage. She was a single person, and these were four young children with complex needs and significant trauma. Even as a couple, we found it incredibly challenging to meet all their needs. While none of the children had formal diagnoses at the time, they each showed signs that pointed towards future diagnoses. It took both of us working together—tag teaming, coordinating, supporting each other—to provide them with the care and attention they needed. How could one person, with limited support around her, realistically manage that?

During the visit, we left the children with her for just a couple of hours at another time. When we returned, she was visibly exhausted. She shook her head and let out a tired sigh. "I don't know how you do it, and there's *two* of you."

I nodded internally. Of course. It was hard for us, even with the two of us working together. How could she possibly handle all four on her own?

AT THIS POINT, it seemed certain that the siblings would stay together in our care. Then, out of the blue one day, I got a call saying that restoration to the father seemed possible for Sally. I was dumbfounded. *Where had this come from? For the past 18 months, we'd been told restoration wasn't even an option for this parent. Now, they were seriously considering splitting this child from her siblings?* My mind was racing, and my frustration rose.

As the weeks passed, the picture became clearer. Restoration for Sally wasn't just a possibility—it was a very real potential. The agency requested that we make her available for more family contact, which we agreed to, but it broke my heart to think of her being separated from her siblings.

Sally's birth father was always consistent with his contact visits, but each time she returned, she was completely dysregulated and loaded up on junk food. He struggled to set boundaries with her, unable to say no.

We were increasingly concerned about her well-being. She had severe eczema and exhibited signs of autism, and her behaviours after visits were escalating. The aftermath weighed heavily on us.

We had met him a few times—he was a nice guy, kind and well-meaning. But kindness alone wasn't enough. Did he truly have the capacity to care for a four-year-old with complex needs?

When all four children were placed with us, it felt like there was a chance we might keep them all together. But as is so often the case in foster care, there were so many moving parts and so much uncertainty. Sally's birth father had initially been denied, but he got a lawyer and fought fiercely for his child. While it saddened us to think of the siblings being split, I couldn't deny the love that he showed through his determination.

———

ONE AFTERNOON, our little girl, Sally, twirled around the house, singing joyfully, "We're staying with Sam and Dani forever!" over and over again.

I wanted so badly to say, "Yes, sweetheart, you are." But I couldn't.

The truth was, we had no idea what the future held. Months of uncertainty still loomed ahead, and no matter how much I wished to give her the stability she craved, the decision wasn't mine to make.

Watching her dance, so blissfully unaware of the unknowns, my heart ached. She deserved certainty. She deserved forever.

———

THIS JOURNEY HAS BEEN FILLED with emotional highs and lows. So many times, we've thought one moment they'd stay with us forever, only for the next to bring news that they might leave. And we're not alone in this experience—most foster carers face this kind of uncertainty.

I met a couple who took in a sibling group of two for what was meant to be a weekend respite. Three years later, the children are still with them. That's the unpredictable reality of foster care.

———

ANOTHER ONE of the biggest challenges of being a foster carer is learning to navigate the system. Everyone says, "It's broken," but once you're in it, you truly see just how broken it is. It can feel overwhelming and nearly impossible to understand at first. Over time, though, you start to learn how it works—or doesn't—and find ways to manage within it.

I've been on both sides: being a foster carer and working within the system in various capacities. These dual experiences have taught me a lot about what it takes to be part of this challenging yet rewarding world.

In my position, while working at one of the foster care agencies, I began doing assessments of potential foster carers. Having experienced the assessment process both as a foster carer and as a worker, I often feel a mixture of compassion for carers and conflict about the process itself. Each agency conducts assessments differently, but the commonality is that they are often lengthy and deeply invasive, scrutinising every aspect of a carer's life. It can feel as though they're more focused on uncovering flaws than recognising strengths.

A couple reached out to become foster carers, and I was assigned their case. The couple seemed ideal. They were middle-aged, with two well-adjusted children, stable jobs in the community sector, and a spacious five-bedroom home. They were motivated by a genuine desire to help children in need, and their flexibility and understanding of the system seemed like assets. Their assessment felt straightforward—no red flags, no doubts. I was confident presenting them to the panel.

To my surprise, the panel scrutinised them. They questioned the couple's decision to continue working, even though their jobs allowed significant flexibility. They also took issue with the couple's preference for children younger than their own, which I saw as a protective measure for their family. The panel's focus on these details felt counterproductive, especially considering the chronic shortage of carers in the out-of-home care system. Questioning such capable people seemed impractical. The couple got approved in the end, but the scrutiny seemed unnecessary.

This experience brought me back to my own assessment process. The panel was doing to them what I felt happened to us. Rather than focusing on our potential as carers, it often felt like the agency was searching for reasons to doubt us. While I understand the importance of thorough assessments, the process can be demoralising for those of us who have faced life's challenges but still want to provide a safe and loving home for children in foster care.

There are undoubtedly stories of unsuitable carers that justify the system's caution. The fear of placing children in the wrong environment is valid. However, the process can feel alienating to "normal" people who, despite imperfect histories, are willing to give children the care they deserve. One day, a colleague admitted to me, "I wouldn't pass this process." She was a capable, compassionate woman with a stable family, but her life wasn't flawless. Whose is?

Going through the assessment process is challenging, but it's absolutely achievable. Looking back, I wish I had a clearer understanding of what to expect before starting the journey. Even the most seemingly perfect carers will face scrutiny—it's just part of the process.

If you're going through it, do your best not to take it personally. As unfair or frustrating as it may feel at times, it's simply how the system operates.

That's part of my motivation for writing this book—to equip prospective foster carers with the tools, insights, and realistic expectations they need before embarking on this journey.

ONE AFTERNOON, we received a call from our caseworker that she was transferring our case to a different caseworker. Our first one, while challenging at times, generally treated us with respect, expressed gratitude for what we were doing, and genuinely tried to support us.

Our new caseworker was Chloe.

Chloe was young—new to the role. From what we observed, her lack of experience impacted the way the case was handled, which in turn affected the children and us. Although I'm well aware that caseworkers are overloaded with case files, things often fell through the cracks. Also, Chloe wasn't a parent, and although it isn't a qualifying factor to be a good caseworker, it does impact their ability to understand our role and support us. From our perspective and based on our experience, she lacked an understanding of the day-to-day realities of raising kids, the little things that can make all the difference.

To her credit, Chloe was polite. She was kind when she spoke to us. But kindness only goes so far. The real challenge was the lack of communication—decisions made without consulting us, plans put in place without a conversation. And in foster care, where stability and collaboration are everything, that made working with her incredibly frustrating.

Sometimes, the decisions made by the agency left me fuming. They feel thoughtless—made in a vacuum, without real consultation or genuine consideration for the well-being of the kids. And then, we're simply informed of what's happening, as if our role in their daily lives doesn't matter.

WE DON'T OFTEN MAKE requests. We get on with our role as foster carers, doing as much as we can independently, without agency intervention. But there are limits to this.

Scotty, now 18 months, and Siera, just 3, were seeing their parents for four-hour visits—plus a 45-minute drive each way with a worker. These long visits were emotionally and physically draining for such young children. They missed their midday naps, returned overtired and overstimulated, and were often unsettled for days afterwards. While they enjoyed seeing their parents, they had minimal attachment to them, and no consistent connection with the caseworkers who supervised the visits either.

Our issue with the length of contact wasn't about denying the birth parents time—it was about the developmental and psychological impact on the children. Stability and security are fundamental to raising well-adjusted children. So is routine. When young children are pulled out of their rhythms—transported long distances by strangers to spend hours with people they barely know—it disrupts their ability to form healthy attachments. For children already removed from their primary caregivers, building secure connections with their current carers is vital. Disrupting that bond for contact that exceeds even the court's order of two hours does more harm than good.

I sent a polite email requesting a reduction—not to eliminate contact, but to make it more appropriate for the children's age and stage. Weeks passed with no response. Then finally, a text:

"We cannot change them. They will remain the same," Chloe wrote.

That was it.

What made it more difficult was that final orders had already been made—the parents had lost their legal rights. And that doesn't happen easily. While I carry deep empathy for the birth parents, knowing they too came from trauma and hardship, I also know that these children now needed someone to fight for *them*. To ensure that their pain didn't continue the cycle of harm.

———

EVERY DECISION MADE from this point forward should have centred the child's best interests—not the adults'. Secure attachment to a consistent, responsive caregiver is one of the strongest protective factors in a child's development. Contact visits, while important, must be shaped with this in mind. Yes, birth parents should be given the opportunity to remain connected—but only within the boundaries of what supports the child's healing.

Too often, I've seen the opposite: children terrified of seeing their birth parents, refusing to go, and being forced anyway. Pressuring a child to visit someone who has hurt them isn't therapeutic—it's retraumatising. We need to rethink how we support the child, how we honour the birth family *without putting the parents' needs above the child's*. It's not about severing ties. It's about creating safety. We owe these kids more than blanket policies. We owe them nuanced, child-focused care.

Even though I knew the kids in my care might not be with me forever, I couldn't just let go when I saw decisions being made that weren't in their best interest. I wasn't trying to stop them from seeing their parents. I wasn't trying to keep them. I just wanted to protect them.

It often feels like they don't truly care about the children we're entrusted to nurture and protect. For them, it's a job—a checklist to complete, a report to file. As long as everything looks good on paper and their manager is satisfied, they're content. Meanwhile, we're the ones living the reality of these decisions, picking up the pieces when they fall apart. And yet, we're treated as an afterthought. A quick text is all we get—no respect for our role, no recognition of the emotional and physical labour we pour into these children. It can be infuriating.

AT TIMES, it feels like an abusive relationship. So why continue? Because, despite it all, I love these kids. The system is flawed, but my commitment to the children keeps me going. When a bad decision is made, I allow myself to feel it. I get angry, I vent, I yell, and sometimes I swear. But after that, I remind myself why I'm here: for the kids. I can't and won't stop advocating for them, even when the system frustrates me beyond belief.

Over time, I've learned to put things into perspective. When my caseworker frustrates me, I remind myself that they often have little real power. They're caught in the middle, trying to follow orders handed down from their manager, who is often just following directives from higher up. Government policies and political priorities beyond anyone's immediate control shape many of these decisions.

In an ideal world, we'd all agree on what's best for the child. But we live in a complex, imperfect system, and that's not the reality. Disagreements with the agency are inevitable. You'll be angry, sometimes livid, at their choices. But you have to find ways to manage that anger and frustration. Know when to stand your ground and when to let it go. You can't control every outcome, but you can control how you respond.

EVENTUALLY, I found myself overwhelmed by the weight of our situation, so I reached out to a local psychologist for support. She has been a lifesaver for me. She hasn't fixed my situation, but she has helped me manage better and consider what I can control. Another strategy I started to engage more was leaning on other carers for support and a much-needed rant. If you are finding yourself in the same position, find what works for you, because you will disagree with the agency, and it will be hard. But it's part of the journey, and learning to navigate these challenges is crucial for your well-being and for the kids in your care.

Working within the agencies gave me another perspective on the system. It revealed layers of complexity and often left me questioning where the common sense had gone. My colleague and I leaned on each other daily, helping one another navigate the challenges of the job.

One day, we were both thrilled to hear that a childless couple —an accountant and a teacher—had been approved as foster carers through our agency. But when their approval came through, our excitement quickly turned to frustration. They were only approved for one child under the age of two. The couple hadn't set this limit themselves—the panel had. In reality, they were open to siblings and older children, but the decision had been made for them.

My colleague and I exchanged knowing looks. *"They won't get a match for ages,"* she sighed. I nodded.

With the current climate, most young children are prioritised for restoration with their birth families during their early years. The unfortunate reality was that this couple—so eager to provide a home—would likely be left waiting. While placements for young, single children do come up, they are rare. More often, it's older children and sibling groups who need care.

This situation is more common than people realise. One evening, at a community event, I met another carer who had been approved for six months and was still waiting for a placement. It happens all the time—carers go through the lengthy and invasive approval process, only to sit idle for months without a child being placed with them. But this doesn't reflect a lack of children needing homes—there are many in urgent need of a placement. The issue lies in systemic inefficiencies, not in the demand for safe and loving homes.

WHY DOES THIS HAPPEN? The reasons are complex.

For some agencies, it's a matter of capacity—they're hesitant to take on more placements due to limited resources. In other cases, a lack of casework staff means there simply aren't enough workers to manage additional placements. Internal policies, bureaucratic red tape, and logistical challenges within agencies can also prevent children from being placed with available carers.

Carers are left feeling confused and frustrated. They hear the media campaigns desperately calling for more foster carers, yet after being approved, they sit waiting—ignored, overlooked, and without explanation. The disconnect is staggering. The system is anything but transparent, and it is far from well-coordinated.

The lack of collaboration between agencies exacerbates the problem. Agencies often act in competition rather than cooperation. One day in the office, a colleague mentioned that their agency views another one as a competitor. *Why? Shouldn't all agencies be working together to find homes for children?* I thought to myself.

I've seen firsthand how poor communication between agencies leads to missed opportunities—opportunities that could change a child's life.

One afternoon over coffee, I spoke with a friend who was a

foster carer. She had recently taken in a five-year-old who was on the verge of being placed in a hotel, even though they hadn't planned on taking another child. Meanwhile, the agency I was working with had an approved couple eagerly waiting for a child of that age, ready to provide a stable, loving home.

If the two agencies had simply communicated, that child might have gone directly into a forever home instead of facing yet another uncertain placement.

It doesn't make sense—none of it does. If you're an approved carer waiting for a placement, know this: it's not you. The system is flawed, inefficient, and poorly coordinated. At times, it's frustrating and disheartening, but the issue lies with the system, not with your willingness or capability as a carer.

WORKING within the foster care system often feels like navigating a storm. The challenges can feel endless: invasive assessments, lack of transparency, constant disagreements, and systemic inefficiencies. It's frustrating, exhausting, and, at times, disheartening. But it's also important.

The system isn't perfect, but it's the one we have. As carers and agency workers, we have to accept its flaws while working tirelessly to improve it—not just for the children in our care today, but for those who will enter the system tomorrow. That means advocating for better communication, showing respect for everyone involved, and finding ways to support yourself when the system feels overwhelming.

It's not easy, and there will be moments when you question why you keep going. But at the end of the day, the children are the reason we persevere. They are worth every fight, every frustration, and every tear. We may not fix the system overnight, but we can be part of the change it so desperately needs.

Placement Breakdown & Sibling Relationships

The months passed, and life felt stable. We were a solid unit, enjoying the rhythm of our days together. But as time wore on, and two years into the placement, the cracks began to show. The oldest child, Sean, who had grown so much, started to change, and the dynamics of our family began to shift.

Sean became more defiant, his frustration spilling over into constant fights with his siblings. From the beginning, he had always been a lot—high-energy, demanding attention every second of the day. He couldn't sit still long enough to watch a movie, not even for a moment of reprieve. But this was different. This was a new level.

ADDING HIS YOUNGER BROTHER, Scotty, to the mix only intensified his need for attention. He wanted to be treated like him, to be held in the same way, to be given the same type of attention. But he was seven, and with four children in the house, we simply couldn't give him that level of one-on-one care.

He thrived at school, which was a relief, so we enrolled him in after-school care, hoping it would help. And in some ways, it did. But no matter how much we gave, he still needed more than we had to offer.

We tried so hard with him. We tried everything—sticker charts, positive reinforcement, negative reinforcement, hugs and cuddles, one-on-one time, sports, video games—the list goes on. And yet, we still don't know what to do.

He pushes for control, he lies, he constantly demands attention, and he screams. I know he's hurting from a lack of attachment in his early years and forced to live a life of independence from his caregiver far too young. But knowing that doesn't make it any less exhausting for us to handle now.

When he's angry, he makes sure everyone knows it. His logic can be nearly impossible to follow, and if I can't understand his reasoning, it only escalates his frustration.

His birthday was coming up, and I wanted to make it special. I planned the party, carefully picked out the bike he had been asking for, baked the cake, and even set aside the exact outfit he had asked to wear. I wanted everything to feel just right.

When the day arrived, he was beaming with excitement as he tore into his present. For a moment, everything was perfect.

Then, just as quickly, the moment unravelled. Within minutes, he was fighting over toys with his younger siblings. I gently reminded him to share, asking him not to snatch from his sister. But instead of listening, he screamed at me—loud, unrelenting. I told him to take a break, to calm down, but he refused. The tantrum escalated, his defiance pushing against every boundary.

By the time I finally got everyone ready—wrangling kids for school, daycare, and work—I was drained. We made it out the door, and as I slid into my car, I exhaled heavily, gripping the steering wheel.

I had wanted so badly to make this day special for him. But instead, it felt awful.

ONCE HE STARTS, the others follow suit, and suddenly, it's chaos. The younger ones begin crying and screaming, and I feel overwhelmed and triggered, my patience wearing thin. My instinct is to put him down and rush to the younger ones, but when all of them are screaming at once, it's too much. I try to address one problem, and within seconds, there's another. It's an endless, overwhelming cycle.

I tell Siera not to scream—to use her words—but she's too young to understand. Scotty doesn't understand either, and he just screams louder. I know it's not their fault; their behaviour stems from deeper issues. But I simply don't have the time to meet all their needs 100% of the time.

One morning, Sean needed a calm talk after getting into trouble, so I offered him a hug, which he gratefully accepted. Just as I was speaking with him, Scotty started screaming for reasons I couldn't discern. I wanted to comfort Scotty, but I still had to deal with Sean. Once Sean was settled, I went to Scotty and gave him a hug. Then Siera and Sally began to fight over their toys. They all needed me at the same time, and I couldn't be there for all of them simultaneously.

I was feeling overwhelmed often—there was simply too much happening at once. I was constantly trying to manage everyone's needs, and it felt like an impossible task. And on top of it all, I still needed to get ready for work.

DURING THIS TIME, we also shared some wonderful moments with Sean.

One sunny afternoon, I decided to take him out for some one-on-one time. We walked over to the soccer fields; the grass was bright and inviting, and we spent the afternoon kicking the ball around together. He challenged me to races across the field, always insisting he had to win. We laughed together, the sound of his joy momentarily washing away the weight of our struggles. In that simple moment, it felt like everything might be okay.

As we walked home, I found myself thinking, *maybe we can do this. Maybe we can make this work.* Hope stirred in me as I imagined more moments like this.

BUT HOPE IS FRAGILE. That evening, as I set his dinner on the table, he refused to eat. Before I could process his defiance, he threw the plate onto the floor. I took a deep breath, trying to stay calm, and attempted to reason with him. When that failed, my patience crumbled. I lost my cool and told him to go to his room.

But he wouldn't go. He stood his ground, his tiny frame stiff with defiance, screaming at us with a force that belied his age. It became a standoff—neither of us budging.

I was at a loss. I had tried so hard to love this child, pouring so much energy into giving him attention and care. Yet, at that moment, it felt like nothing I did was enough.

WE HAD ALREADY TOLD the agency previously that we weren't managing him very well. We were trying our best, and it wasn't working. We needed help. We reached out to our caseworker, Chloe, who said she would speak to her manager and see what they could do.

Determined to find support, we located a therapist who was ready and willing to take him on. We asked the agency if we could book him in. Their answer was no. They insisted he needed to see one of *their* psychologists. So, we waited—weeks turned into months. And things only got worse.

We pushed again, begging for him to see the agency's psychologist. Finally, she came to our home. I poured my heart out, explaining the struggles and how hard this was on our family. She empathised, acknowledging the difficulty of our situation and thanking us for trying so hard to keep the children together. She promised to follow up and start therapy soon.

But then weeks went by. Silence.

By that time, I'd had enough, I took matters into my own hands and booked Sean in to see my therapist friend. It was amazing—exactly what this child needed. He finally had a space to process, to be seen and heard. But it was too late. We had already reached our breaking point. Therapy like this should have started years ago, not when we were already drowning.

The agency occasionally provided youth workers to give Sean one-on-one support, which eased some of the pressure. But it also felt invasive, having a stranger in our home every night—a constant reminder of how overwhelmed we had become. Their presence gave us a brief reprieve from the relentless sibling fights and made it easier to settle the three younger ones while the youth worker focused on Sean. For a short while, the evenings were a little more manageable.

But it was never enough. It wasn't sustainable. The workers could only do so much, and when they weren't there, the full weight of managing four children fell back on us. Mornings were the worst—trying to get everyone ready and ourselves out the door for work felt impossible.

We reached out to the agency again.

Their advice? Put him in front of an iPad.

"We tried that," I responded. "It only made things worse. He became more defiant, angrier, and even harder to manage."

Sam and I went back and forth. There were moments when we convinced ourselves we could manage, where we clung to the hope that things would improve. But Sam saw the reality more clearly. He knew we couldn't keep going like this.

"We need to call the manager again," he urged me. "They need to do something, or he needs to go. We've asked for help, and it's not enough."

I resisted. I didn't want to make that call. We had tried everything—suggesting therapy, asking for more support so one of us wouldn't have to work, and requesting respite. But nothing impactful materialised. Yes, we were grateful for the workers who stepped in, but it wasn't enough. The strain on our home was undeniable, and deep down, I knew it wasn't working. But knowing it and accepting it were two different things.

I know Sam didn't want to let him go either, but he could see the damage it was causing more clearly than I could.

THAT MORNING, we got ready for work and school, dropped the kids off and parked outside my office building. Before I stepped inside, Sam and I sat together in the car, preparing to make the call. My hands shook. My heart pounded. We knew the manager wouldn't be in until 9 a.m., so we waited, the weight of what we were about to do pressing down on us.

Tears streamed down my face as I finally spoke the words I never thought I would say. "We need to relinquish care of Sean."

I sobbed as I told the manager, "He needs to be moved as soon as possible. We love him—that's what makes this so hard. But we can't do this anymore."

I never thought this would happen. I never imagined reaching a point where I would say that I wanted a child I loved deeply out of my home. I've tried so hard with him, but we can't continue this way.

The agency finally listened. They prepared for his move and told us he would be leaving in two weeks.

When I told him he would be moving, he cried. But mixed with his tears was a glimmer of excitement—he would live with Maria, someone he knew was a part of his family.

THE DAY BEFORE HIS MOVE, his caseworker came to take him out for dinner. When he returned home, something was different. He wasn't himself.

As soon as the door closed behind the caseworker, he burst into tears.

I held him tightly, feeling my heart shatter into a million pieces. *Man, I love this kid.* But I knew—deep down—I couldn't be what he needed anymore. My heart was breaking, but I had to let him go.

I sat on the edge of his bed, settling him in for his final night in our home. He looked small, unsure, a flicker of fear in his eyes. I lay beside him, and he talked the night away. I let him. After everything we'd been through, all I wanted was for him to feel safe, to feel loved.

We talked about his new school, how he'd get to see his mum more, and the possibility of Maria signing him up for a sport. I knew he was nervous, but I wanted to help him see the good, to imagine the possibilities.

"You can come back and visit anytime," I told him, watching his face light up.

"And if you ever get scared, just ask Maria if you can call me."

He snuggled into my arm, his small body pressing close. He had no idea we were the ones asking for him to leave, and we were determined to keep it that way. That burden wasn't his to carry. All he needed to know was that he was loved.

He left the next day. He was quiet. Seemed unsure. We all waved as the caseworker's car pulled out of the driveway. Within the hour, my phone was ringing. It was him on FaceTime. He excitedly showed me the present I had snuck into his bag before he left, and then we said goodbye one more time.

AS THE WEEKS WENT ON, I found myself questioning, "Did I do the right thing?" The home is so much more peaceful, but I miss him so much. He drove me crazy, but my love for him ran deep. I wish I could tell him I love him one more time.

Six months later, we've spoken to him once on FaceTime. I continue to send him packages, but I never hear a response from him or Maria. I just hope that when he receives them, he feels a bit of love.

PLACEMENT BREAKDOWN WAS something we were never truly prepared for. The training touched on it, but not fully. We should have had more support with him. It made me angry that the agency didn't do enough—for him and for us. We asked for respite time again and again, desperate for a break, but the answer was always the same: *there weren't any carers available.* Waiting two years for a psychologist or any kind of meaningful intervention is far too long.

I regret the way things turned out, though I also don't think there was anything more we could have done. The placement was going to end, eventually; we just made it end sooner than it would have. Still, I can't help but wonder—if we had been given the right support sooner, could it have been different? Maybe it still would have ended, maybe not. That uncertainty leaves a hollow ache, a constant "what if."

There are moments I replay in my mind—the times I know I said or did the wrong thing and wish I could take it back. And now, with Maria not supporting ongoing communication, there is no closure. My heart feels shattered, left to hope from a distance that he is safe, that he is healing, and that somehow, he will know he was loved.

As a carer, you want to make it work for the child's sake. You want to help. You push through all the painful moments with the hope that it will work, and you feel like a complete failure when you say the words, "I need to relinquish care." It's not what you want. You went into caring for this child with hopes and expectations, but you can't bear the weight any longer. Either you have a mental breakdown, or the child needs to go. Your home isn't a happy one anymore.

THERE ARE many factors that contribute to a placement breakdown, and it's rarely as simple as a carer "not coping." Unlike biological families, foster carers and children don't start with a built-in bond. That connection has to be formed—often in the context of trauma, uncertainty, and enormous pressure.

One often overlooked factor is temperament—the natural personality traits we are born with. The four children we were matched with for adoption had very gentle temperaments. They were emotionally sensitive, eager to please, and if I so much as raised my voice a decibel, they would cry. Parenting them felt calm, natural, and rewarding.

By contrast, Sean, Sally, Siera and Scotty were strong-willed and intensely defiant. They were emotionally sensitive too, but in a different way—quick to push back, highly independent, and determined to have things their own way. These qualities might one day help them change the world—but in the context of trauma and disrupted attachment, they made parenting an incredibly complex task.

Then, there is trauma itself. The children we were matched with for adoption had endured extreme hardship—trauma that left them longing for safety, family, and connection. Their pain made them cling to us with openness. The four temporary children's trauma, while also painful, expressed itself differently. It shaped them into survivors who had learned to rely on no one. They were guarded, fiercely independent, and had learned that control equals safety. Building trust in that context takes time, consistency, and a level of support we simply weren't given.

AFTER WE SAID goodbye to the three children the first time, I began looking for work. The plan was for me to work part-time while we stayed open to taking in a sibling group of two, knowing I needed to balance work and caring. Maybe down the track we'd open our home to a larger sibling group, but while we were doing temporary care, I also wanted to return to casework for a while. When a part-time role opened at a local foster care agency, I jumped at it.

But then all four children returned to our care—and without warning, we stepped right back into chaos. At the time, we didn't fully realise it. We just loved them. We wanted to be a family. As the chaos escalated, we began to consider me quitting my job to stay home with them. But we didn't have the certainty of tomorrow. We went back and forth. I wanted to resign—but how could I justify leaving another job when we still didn't know if the children would stay?

If we had known the placement would be long-term or permanent, I would have walked away from work in a heartbeat. Caring for four children with complex trauma is not something you can sustainably do on top of a job. These kids needed a full-time parent. But we were stuck in the waiting—waiting for final orders, waiting for clarity. And in that waiting, the toll on our family was immense.

We also had minimal support for Sean, Sally, Siera and Scotty. By contrast, the four children we hoped to adopt came with a network already in place. Despite our issues with their agency, they were proactive about the children's therapeutic needs. The children had NDIS plans, additional funding to support their development, and therapy appointments already underway.

With the second sibling group, we had to start from scratch. No therapy. No extra funding. No structure around us—just us, trying to hold it all together while both working and parenting kids who had significant trauma.

That's why we were so frustrated when Sean's behaviour escalated and help never came. Maybe—*maybe*—with the right therapeutic interventions, and if I hadn't been split between work and caregiving, we could have held the placement together. But we'll never know. And that's part of the grief too—living with the unanswered question: *Could it have been different, if someone had stepped in sooner?*

So, before anyone draws comparisons between placements, or assumes the number of children is all that matters, I would ask them to pause. Because placements don't rise and fall on numbers alone. They are shaped by trauma, temperament, system failures, lack of support, and—most of all—the complex, beautiful, and often painful effort of trying to love children who've been deeply hurt.

A FEW MONTHS after Sean's departure, a fellow foster carer called me. She shared her experience relinquishing care of one of the siblings in her care. Her experience resonated exactly with mine.

"We just couldn't do it anymore," she said. "She needed one-on-one care. It's better for these siblings to be separate."

Sibling relationships in foster care are complicated. At first, I believed it was always best for siblings to stay together. After all, those bonds are among the most formative and enduring in our lives. But over time, I came to realise that sometimes keeping siblings together isn't actually what's best for the children.

For Sean, his trauma had shaped him in ways that made sharing us with his siblings incredibly difficult. What he craved—what he had been denied in his early years—was one-on-one attention. He longed for a parent to himself. When the time came for him to leave his siblings, he didn't seem to mind. Even his therapist remarked how unusual it was that he showed no concern. To Sean, the priority wasn't staying with his siblings; it was finally having parental attention focused on him.

The reality is that trauma can profoundly impact sibling relationships. Sometimes, the deep wounds children carry mean that staying together isn't the healthiest or safest option. For Sean, being apart from his siblings gave him the space he needed to begin healing in a way that wouldn't have been possible otherwise.

Since our experience, I've met other children who have thrived with one-on-one carers. In some cases, children are initially placed with their siblings, but over time, it becomes clear that their individual needs aren't being met in a shared placement. Separating siblings may feel counterintuitive, but sometimes, it's the best way to ensure each child receives the attention and care they require to heal and grow. Hearing these others' stories helped me come to an acceptance of the situation. Maybe he, with his siblings, just wasn't the best option.

FOR SIX MONTHS, it has been just us and the three kids, and things were going well. Life felt settled. We all still missed Sean deeply, but the household was much calmer.

Then came the long-awaited final orders. The kids had been on temporary orders the entire time they had been in our care, but now it was time for the magistrate to make a final ruling on their future.

We waited anxiously for a call from Chloe. Days passed after court before she finally rang.

"The final orders have been made," she said. "Sally is being restored to her birth father, and Siera and Scotty will be moving to Maria's, where their brother Sean is. The only thing is, Maria needs a bigger house to take them, so we'll have to wait to move them until she sorts that out. Sally, however, will be moving within the next few weeks."

I nodded, absorbing the news. We had expected it. It had been clear for some time that they were planning to move the kids on.

I had been emotionally preparing myself for their departure for the past couple of months.

Sally had been seeing her dad every weekend and had built a

good relationship with him. It wasn't as stable or healthy as I had hoped, but there was no doubt he loved her.

When I told her she was going to live with him, she looked at me, confused.

At the airport, I knelt beside her and gently asked, "Are you excited to go live with Daddy?"

"No," she whispered, her wide eyes filled with uncertainty.

My heart clenched. I knew this was hard for her. Would she be okay?

I wanted to hold on, to reassure her, to promise that everything would be fine. But I couldn't. This was happening.

Her dad arrived, thanking us for taking care of her. I watched as they boarded the plane together, a lump forming in my throat.

In the weeks that followed, we received frequent FaceTime calls—her bright little face lighting up the screen, eager to share bits of her new life. It was comforting.

Over time, the calls became less frequent. And as much as I missed her, I knew that was a good thing. It meant she was settling in.

―――

EIGHT MONTHS AFTER SHE LEFT, we finally got to see her in person again. It was a beautiful moment. We stood at the airport, hearts racing with anticipation, waiting for her and her dad to arrive. They were the last two off the plane. As she stepped through the doors and saw our faces through the glass, she broke into a run.

She ran straight into my arms, and I held her tight.

"I love you. I love you. I love you," she said over and over again.

"Oh, I love you too, sweetheart. I've missed you so much."

I gently put her down, and she immediately grabbed my hand. Together, we walked out of the airport.

We spent a few days together—playing at parks, visiting the beach, watching the kids laugh and run around like no time had passed. One afternoon at the beach, I bent down to pick up the lunch bag when I felt two little arms wrap around me from behind.

"I love you," she whispered.

No, I don't get to see her anymore. But I am so grateful I had the chance to be this little girl's mum—even if just for a while. She may not be with me forever, but I will love her as if she were mine for the rest of my life.

The Weight of Waiting

It's just the four of us now—Scotty, now almost 3 years old, and Siera, who is 4.

But we're still living in limbo.

For the past 10 months, whenever we ask if the children are still going to leave our care or stay with us, Chloe tells us the same thing: "The final orders are for them to be with Maria. The decision is determined by the Aboriginal Child Placement principles."

The Aboriginal Child Placement principles are a set of guidelines that aim to preserve and support the cultural identity of Aboriginal and Torres Strait Islander children in foster care. It highlights the importance of placing children with kin and community where possible. This sounds beautiful in theory. But in practice, it's rarely straightforward. Just because a child has Aboriginal heritage doesn't automatically mean that being placed with kin is the best option in every case.

Before I continue, I want to stop here and make it clear that I don't claim to know everything. I believe the Aboriginal Child Placement Principles were created by well-meaning people who wanted to ensure that Aboriginal children receive the best possible care—care that nurtures their identity, maintains their cultural connections, and helps heal the wounds left by the past.

But applying a blanket principle to deeply complex situations can lead to unintended harm.

Recently, I spoke with a proud Aboriginal woman and shared our story with her. "Connection to culture is what matters most," she said. Her words comforted me. I truly believe we honoured that. We've worked hard to maintain connection with the children's birth family and culture. But we were told it wasn't enough—that the children must be on Country, with kin, even when there were significant and well-founded concerns about the stability of the placement and the children's future wellbeing.

We need culturally safe, trauma-informed practices. I'm not against the Aboriginal Child Placement Principles—I support the intent behind them—but when they're applied without nuance, children suffer. These children are more than their heritage. They are complex humans with their own history, trauma, attachments, developmental needs and personalities.

I believe it's essential that we regularly reflect on all the principles, policies, and procedures we use in child protection—regardless of their origin or intent. The Aboriginal Child Placement Principles, like many others in the system, were created with important goals in mind, and I deeply respect their intention to preserve culture and identity. But no principle should ever be applied blindly. When any guideline—cultural, legal, or procedural—overlooks a child's existing attachments, dismisses carer insights, or fails to consider the unique needs of the individual child, we risk causing harm. In such a complex space, we need thoughtful, case-by-case approaches that truly prioritise the best interests of children.

EACH TIME we followed up with Chloe for more information on the children's long-term placement, we ask the same question: "When?"

But she never has an answer. It could be two weeks, four months, a year—or, as every carer knows, it could be forever.

Forever seems unlikely in this case, though. And that uncertainty—the weight of an unknown future—hangs over us every single day.

Some days, I feel prepared for it. I feel as if I have learned to deal with the limbo and am impressed by my coping skills. But then I get an email. An email I thought I was prepared for but was not.

"We are making progress." Chloe gives an update that Maria is progressing in her situation, getting ready for the children to arrive. My heart sinks. This is reality. She's actually getting ready. The reality of them leaving is getting closer. Man, it hurts. My chest is tight, thinking of letting them go. They are my babies. They are my world. I don't want them to go. Tears fill my eyes as I once again process them leaving. Sitting while taking deep breaths, I process this loss all over again.

I DON'T WANT them to go, but I also want a date for when they're going—it would be easier to know, so I can finally process the loss. While I'm stuck in this time of waiting, not knowing when they'll leave, it just hurts over and over again. Every time I'm reminded they're going, it feels like a stab to the heart. I'd rather just rip the band-aid off, cry, and start to move on.

Accepting the outcome you don't believe is the best one for the child is brutal. Everyone can see it. We know it, but it cannot be. The child is stuck in this system, which will determine their future, and it will not be the best. We knew where they were going was not dangerous in a physical sense, but it would not provide the best care they could have. They had an amazing home here with great support and access to family contact.

We communicated to Chloe whenever we spoke of the topic that it was not best for the children, but she would not hear.

SAYING GOODBYE IS NEVER EASY. Even Sean, whom I requested to be removed, was still extremely hard to say goodbye to. It's especially difficult when the kids want to stay with us forever. These kids loved being in our home, and we loved having them. They saw their birth family, but they were always excited to come back home to us.

When you enter the world of temporary care, goodbye is part of the job. It is something you need to get used to, and I do believe you will get used to it. Initially, it's so difficult that you don't think your heart can manage the grief. But as time goes on and you experience it over and over, it becomes manageable. It doesn't mean you don't grieve. It doesn't mean you don't cry and wish they would stay, but it's not as overwhelming as it was. I never thought I'd be able to handle the goodbyes, and no, I don't like them, but I can handle them now.

WE NEEDED to transfer offices as we moved to a different region during the fostering process. We've now met with the new office staff, and we are on their books. We have said we will take temporary children while we still have these two in our care and would take another sibling group when they leave. A call could come at any time, day or night. We won't say yes to anyone, as boundaries, as we've learned, are very important. But our phones are on, and we wait for more unknowns.

It's a strange feeling to love your kids so much while also being slightly excited for the next kids to come. I don't think everyone can do that. I didn't think I could have only a couple of years ago. But now, although the thought of my kids leaving is incredibly sad, I have a little excitement for the next call. What will the kids be like? Will they be boys or girls? What will their temperament be like? Will they stay forever? Or just a short while? Knowing there are thousands of kids out there who need a home and many more to come into the system and knowing I'm in a position to help those kids, is exciting. Now, don't get me wrong, it's terrible. Kids should never go through this. But they do. And I can be there for them. Anyone who is not a foster carer might think I'm crazy. But maybe that's what makes me cut out for this lifestyle.

WHILE WE WAITED to find out the long-term plan for Siera and Scotty, we remained on the agency's list to provide emergency care when needed. One afternoon, I was out working—driving back from seeing a client—when my phone rang. It was our agency contact.

"Hey Dani—I'll get straight to the point. We've got two young girls at the local hospital. Are you able to take them tonight?"

"Let me check with Sam, but it shouldn't be a problem."

I hung up and called Sam immediately.

"Uh, yes," he said. "We'll just need to build the beds that are still in storage... and we don't have a cot—we'll need to go buy one."

"I won't be home until they arrive. Can you set up the bedrooms on your own?"

"Yeah, I'll get it done."

I rang our agency contact back. "We'll take them." They thanked me and promised to keep us updated on their arrival time.

When I got home, Sam was already prepping with the help of our two little ones. "Mummy!" they yelled as I walked in the door. I gave them a big hug, then looked to Sam for an update.

"Just need the sheets on the beds," he said.

I jumped into action. As I made the beds, Siera stood beside me and said, "She can stay with us forever." Her innocence was disarming. Even in her young mind, she could sense how important it was to offer a home—without fully understanding how precarious her own situation still was.

"The caseworker's here!" Sam called out.

I tucked in the last corner of the sheet, ran downstairs, slipped on my shoes, and stepped out into the driveway.

The 8-year-old girl stood sobbing beside the car. "It's been a long day," the caseworker said gently, handing me their backpacks. The younger one, just 12 months old, was being lifted out of the car seat by the support worker.

"Come on inside, everyone," I said softly, leading them into the house.

While I spoke with the caseworker, the four children began playing together. Having our two already at home made it a little easier—the girls felt less alone, and Zali, the older girl, warmed up surprisingly quickly.

The caseworkers left, and just like that, we had two more children in our home—with only two outfits each and a world of big emotions.

That first week, we didn't sleep.

The baby, Mia, had never slept alone, so if she wasn't being held, she cried. Zali, the 8-year-old wasn't much different. She was anxious, unsettled, and needed constant reassurance.

But slowly, things improved. By the end of the week, we had both girls in a solid sleep routine, and the whole household breathed easier.

They stayed just four weeks—but what a beautiful four weeks they were.

TOWARD THE END of their time with us, I found a poem Zali had written:

"There was a girl who had no one beside her.
Only her little sister.
Her mum was not doing so well,
So then her and her little sister went to a foster home
And found her light."
She didn't want to leave. She had found love, and she knew it.
And we loved her. We would've kept her if we could. But she had family—family who wanted her, who were ready to step up. It wasn't perfect, but it was the right move for her and her sister.
We'll miss them. We'll never forget them.
Like every child who comes through our door, a little piece of us went with them. And a little piece of them stayed with us.

SIERA AND SCOTTY have been with us for years. To them, we are "Mama" and "Dada." We've worked hard to support their family contact, ensuring they stay connected to their roots, because we believe in the importance of maintaining those ties. But the thought of them leaving is heartbreaking. We believe the best outcome for them is to stay in the home they know and love, the one where they feel safe and supported. Even their birth mum and dad have expressed that they want the children to remain with us—they can see what's best for their kids. But the agency remains immovable in their decision.

So, while we wait for the inevitable, we focus on loving them. Each day, we pour everything we have into these children, knowing that when they leave, a piece of our hearts will go with them.

ONE AFTERNOON, my sister called. "You need to come home. It looks like this is the end for Mum."

I booked a flight a few days later and made my way back to my hometown. I didn't want to go—not because I didn't want to see my mum, but because I didn't want to leave the kids.

Sam dropped me at the airport, and I rushed through the check-in. Finding a quiet corner, I sank into a chair, tilting my head back as tears filled my eyes.

How am I supposed to say goodbye forever when I can't even bear to say goodbye for a week? I thought to myself.

There are days when I feel like I can't keep going in this life we've chosen. The constant uncertainty, the back-and-forth, the comings and goings, and the lack of acknowledgment for how difficult it all is—it takes a toll. Living with such profound uncertainty is an immense challenge. The heartbreak we endure time and time again is anything but easy. People often say, "I don't know how you do it." The truth is, we're not saints or superheroes; we're just ordinary people trying to navigate this path. We simply believe in these kids more than we fear the pain. There are many tears—at least for me. Some weeks, I find myself crying several times. But somehow, we carry on. We love these kids too much to do anything else.

"You could probably apply for a change of orders," a worker mentioned casually one day.

"Yeah, I guess," I responded, but I didn't think much more about it.

But Sam did.

The next day, he came to me, his expression serious. "What do we need to do? Can we fight this?"

I shrugged, brushing it off. "I don't know." I had already prepared my heart for their departure—I couldn't let myself hope for something that felt impossible.

A few weeks later, we took a rare walk alone, the quiet giving us space to talk. After a long pause, he finally said, "I think I want to fight the decision." His voice was steady, but there was an urgency in his words. "I feel like it would be neglect on my part if I don't do anything. Tearing these kids away from the only family they know, to someone who doesn't have the capacity—it's wrong."

I hesitated, sharing my concerns—the reality of caring for children with Aboriginal and Torres Strait Islander heritage, the complexities of their case, the policies, the weight of it all. But as he spoke, he made a point I couldn't ignore.

"Could you live with the decision if we didn't at least try?"

I swallowed hard. Could I?

Maybe they would still go. Maybe nothing would change. But at least we would know we had done everything in our power to fight for what was truly in their best interest.

THAT EVENING, I sat with Scotty in my arms, his lullabies playing softly in the background. As the familiar tune filled the room, I began to sing along.

"You are my sunshine, my only sunshine. You make me happy when skies are grey. You'll never know, dear, how much I love you… So please don't take my sunshine away."

My voice wavered as tears welled in my eyes. I held him closer, pressing my cheek against his soft hair, savouring the moment—knowing how precious, how fleeting, it might be. We needed to try to appeal the court's decision.

OUR NEXT STEP was to make a formal complaint. We needed to outline our concerns to upper management. For nearly three years, we had endured ongoing issues with how the case, the children, and we as carers were treated—but we stayed quiet, complying with their requests even when we had significant concerns. Yes, we raised some of these concerns with the caseworker from time to time, but they consistently fell on deaf ears. Now, it was time to take things higher.

Our main complaints? That the needs of the children were not being properly considered. That the caseworker—who hardly knew the children—was still making key decisions about their lives. That there was a glaring issue: the children had no meaningful attachment to the relative being considered for placement, and that relative clearly lacked the capacity to care for three children with significant trauma and complex needs.

We outlined our concerns in several clear points, backing each one with evidence. None of it was about us. It was entirely about what was best for the children. Would they listen? Probably not. But we had the facts.

A local friend had experience from when she took her own case—and that of the children in her care—to court. In her situation, it was painfully clear that returning the children to their birth family would be unsafe. Yet the child protection team continued to push for restoration. Meanwhile, the children's trauma worsened by the day. Thankfully, she fought hard, and the judge ultimately ruled in the children's best interests.

Because of her determination, those children were protected. But she shouldn't have had to fight so hard. Acting in the best interests of children doesn't happen automatically—it requires carers who are willing to stand in the gap for the ones they're entrusted to protect.

She had the experience and the know-how. So, I reached out.

"Can we grab a coffee?" I texted her that evening.

Reflections

This isn't the end of the story. As I write, we're in the midst of this incredibly challenging season—riding the rollercoaster day by day. We continue to hope for the best outcome for the children in our care.

The challenges of foster care can be overwhelming. The constant grief and loss weigh heavily. Placement breakdowns are emotionally draining. Asking for support and not receiving it creates feelings of helplessness. There is confusion over the disparity between what the media portrays and the realities that foster carers face. Family contact can be complex, and the system often fails to provide children with the best outcomes. Despite these struggles, we persist, knowing the importance of what we do.

Amidst the challenges, there have also been so many joys: the cuddles my little ones give me, seeing them learning who they are, building a bond with them, giving them love, knowing that they love being in our home, being a mum, giving them life-changing experiences and fun, and seeing our own growth—although extremely painful, still rewarding.

Being a non-Indigenous carer to Aboriginal and Torres Strait Islander people's children also comes with unique challenges and complexities. I once asked my caseworker, "Would it be wrong if I told workers not to place Aboriginal children with us?" It wasn't because I didn't care for or love children who are Aboriginal and Torres Strait Islanders—it was because the injustices I witnessed felt overwhelming. As non-Indigenous carers for Aboriginal children, we face limitations that create uncertainty for both us and the children.

I believe there is also a misconception that having Aboriginal and Torres Strait Islander children in non-Indigenous foster homes is akin to the Stolen Generations. But it's not the same. The Stolen Generations involved the systematic removal of children to erase their culture and assimilate them. As foster carers, we are providing homes for children who have been removed from unsafe situations—not stealing them. This distinction is critical, but as non-Indigenous carers, we often feel silenced, afraid to advocate for the children in our care for fear of being labelled racist. This label feels deeply unfair when our only goal is to provide a loving, stable environment for the children, regardless of their heritage.

I want to acknowledge the incredible importance of culture, identity and community for Aboriginal children. While I don't pretend to fully understand the deep pain caused by the Stolen Generations, I deeply respect the fight for self-determination and culturally safe care. My experiences as a non-Indigenous carer have at times brought me into tension with the system—not because I don't value culture, but because I've struggled to reconcile policy with the individual needs of the children I've come to love. I believe we can hold both truths: that culture matters deeply, and that secure attachments to carers matter too. My hope is to be part of a conversation where we ask: what would it look like to truly prioritise children—in their culture, with their families and in stable homes that meet *all* of their needs?

It's possible to be a non-Indigenous carer to Aboriginal and

Torres Strait Islander children while respecting and embracing their culture. Providing a stable home doesn't mean disregarding their identity—it means working to ensure they maintain connections to their culture and community while also prioritising their safety and well-being. However, prioritising placements solely based on heritage rather than the individual needs of the child risks perpetuating cycles of harm.

I'M SO grateful that we have a positive relationship with our children's birth family. But, understandably, it wasn't easy in the beginning.

During one of our first FaceTime calls with a family member, we were blindsided. "I want those children out of your home now!" they shouted. "They need to be with family!"

I was stunned. My heart pounded as I searched for the right words. "It's not our decision," I said calmly, though inside, I felt shaken. But more than that, I felt for the children, sitting in our home, hearing those words from their own family, words that could make them feel like they didn't belong anywhere.

I feel for the family member who yelled those words. These children were taken from her family. That loss runs deep. I can't pretend to understand what she has lived through, or what she's still carrying. Alongside the intergenerational trauma of the Stolen Generations, her family is fractured.

How it got to this point is complex—mental health, addiction, poverty, pain. Whatever the reasons, she's hurting. We all are. She's grieving a family torn apart. We're trying to hold these children together. Their birth parents are dealing with the loss and involvement of child protection. The stakes are high for all of us.

Over time, things began to shift. Just recently, we attended a family birthday, and the atmosphere couldn't have been more different. As we walked in, I hugged the children's birth mother, and warm smiles greeted us from across the room.

We encouraged the kids to spend time with different family members—some they had never met before. No, we weren't of the same cultural background, but that didn't matter. In that moment, we had built a bridge between two worlds. We all stood together, united by one common goal—to love these kids.

We must move toward a more balanced approach—one that respects culture and heritage but doesn't lose sight of what's best for each child as an individual. Addressing the effects of the Stolen Generations should mean breaking cycles of trauma, not reinforcing them through well-meaning but misguided decisions.

THERE HAVE BEEN countless moments throughout our journey when I thought about giving up and times when I questioned whether I was truly cut out for this role. I loved the idea of being a foster carer, but the reality was far more challenging than I had imagined. Even so, I can honestly say now that I wouldn't trade it for anything.

I love being a foster carer. I love the lessons these kids have taught me and the person I'm becoming through this journey. I love pouring my heart into them and holding onto the hope that it makes a difference in their lives. I look forward to welcoming the next child into my arms and witnessing the incredible transformation that a safe, loving home can bring.

People often ask me, "How do you do it?" with a kind of awe in their voice. The truth is, you just do. You get up each day, and when your heart breaks, you get up again. The kids keep coming, and as much as I grieve and hurt, I wouldn't trade this life without them. They are worth every ounce of the pain.

Building bonds with these children is beautiful. Unlike having a child of your own who has that biological bond, this bond takes time. But once you start seeing the evidence of the bond forming, it's amazing. Finally, they snuggle into your shoulder for protection. Finally, they run to you for a hug when they get hurt. Finally, they call you "mum," knowing you're their safe place.

Sean used to write us love letters. He would write how much he loved us and loved living with us. We had had our ups and downs, he and I, but I really did love him to bits. He always wanted to go back to his family from the moment he arrived. Unlike the other siblings, you could see it in him—a strong desire to return to family. But he also had this love of living with us. We provided him with something he hadn't received before, and he liked it. His mum wasn't able to provide him with the love we gave. His mum had struggles of her own she couldn't overcome, and it left him to be his own parent when he was with her. When we came along, we provided lots of hugs, play, and quality time. We tried to give him everything he didn't have. Now granted, he didn't always appreciate it because of his trauma, but by these little love letters, we were reminded we were doing a good job, even if it didn't fix everything.

Our memories with these kids help us keep going, too. After a long trip, Sam, I, and the four kids were driving in the car on our way home, and one of them asked for music. We put on "Let it Go" from Frozen and blasted it. We all sang and danced together. What a simple but beautiful moment. I was just so grateful in that moment for them in my life.

We're changed forever by the little people who come into our lives. They put their stamp on our hearts, and that will never change. They have taught us lessons that, although challenging to learn, have made us grow in new ways. We are better people because of them. We have learned things that have made us change for the better. We talk a lot about how the carers help kids in care, but not a lot about how the kids help the carers. The kids have helped us so much. And no, that's not why we do it, but I sure am grateful.

I love being a mum to these kids. Some days, I complain, and it's so hard, but I still love it and wouldn't have it any other way.

I'VE HEARD many stories since becoming a foster carer. As I've been told these stories, it's stirred in me the desire to share them. I believe it's important for people to know what really takes place in the foster care industry. They market and advertise beautiful stories to pull people in, but those who have been hurt along the road are often left unheard. I don't share to scare people off, but to shine a light on a system that needs to change. A system that has caused so many people to turn their backs on it because of the damage it has caused. Kids and carers are desperate for change.

The Child Taken Without Goodbye

> A former carer shared her story with me. She had fostered two Aboriginal children who were removed from her care because of their heritage, despite forming deep attachments. One of these children was with her from birth until age five. Then, one afternoon, without warning, a caseworker picked the child up from school and placed him with a family who identified as Aboriginal. There were no goodbyes, no transition—he was simply gone.
>
> Years later, the child found her. He told her he'd moved between multiple foster homes, ending in a youth residential home and asked, "Why didn't you want to keep me?" With tears in her eyes, she explained she had wanted to but wasn't allowed to. His response was devastating: "So, because of racism, I didn't get a mum?"

The Abrupt Grandparent Placement

> Another carer told me she could no longer foster after her

experience. She had cared for two young siblings for two years. During that time, she was repeatedly told they would never return to their birth family. The grandparents were denied placement several times due to safety concerns. But suddenly, after years of rejection, they were approved. The children were removed abruptly and placed with their grandparents. The carer was so heartbroken by the loss that she couldn't bear to open her heart again.

The Broken Adoption Promise

A child's birth mother had specifically chosen one couple to care for a baby girl. They wanted the childless couple to adopt her as their own. Six months later, the birth mother unexpectedly changed her mind and regained custody despite being in no position to care for the child. The couple was left heartbroken and questioning the fairness of the system.

The Young Couple's Redemption

Another young couple we met dreamed of adopting. After enduring the challenges of the assessment process, they were placed with a sibling group of two needing a forever home. After six months in their care, the courts decided the children would be returned to their birth family. But when the children were restored to their birth family, the wife experienced a mental breakdown. The emotional toll of the loss was nearly unbearable. Thankfully, a few months later, they were placed with two young children whom they were able to adopt two years later, finding joy after so much heartache.

The Promise That Never Came

A couple I spoke with had cared for two children from birth. For three years, they were the only parents those children knew. Then, out of nowhere, the agency informed them the kids would be moved to a distant relative—because it was kin, it was deemed best. The couple was heartbroken. The children were too young to understand. The agency promised a slow transition: regular visits to build attachment and continued contact after the move. But none of it happened. The children left without bonding with the relative, and after that day, there was no contact—no visits, no updates. The couple grieved deeply, especially for the children, who must have felt abandoned by the only family they had ever known.

Cultural Injustice in Adoption

Another carer shared her heartbreaking experience of fostering an Aboriginal child from birth. She also fostered a non-Indigenous child from birth. The non-Indigenous child was adopted as soon as it was legally allowed, but the Aboriginal child was not. Despite the child asking her foster mum often, "Can I be adopted too?" the system prevented it. That child's sense of security wasn't considered, leaving a painful gap in what should have been a stable, loving home.

THESE ARE JUST a few of the realities families face in Australia's foster care system. The stories I've shared—along with countless others—need to be heard if we're to see the true picture of foster care in Australia.

As someone living through that heartbreak, I've learned that the lack of positive stories doesn't make the journey any less worthwhile. More often than not, the hardest things in life are the ones most worth doing. I'm so grateful that in the moments when I felt like giving up, I didn't. That I kept getting up and trying, even when it felt impossible.

Deep down, I know that even though I'm far from perfect, the love I give these kids will leave a lasting impact. My hope is that these stories, while difficult to hear, will inspire those working within the foster care system to strive for positive change. Together, we can work toward a system where more positive stories emerge—stories of healing, stability, and hope.

For anyone feeling discouraged by these challenges, remember that difficulty doesn't make something any less valuable. If anything, it's proof of how much it matters.

Foster care is not easy. It is filled with grief, uncertainty, and challenges. But it is also filled with joy, growth, and moments of profound connection. We are forever changed by the children who come into our lives. Their resilience, love, and lessons shape us into better people. Though saying goodbye is never easy, it is a testament to the bonds we build and the love we provide. And so, we continue, knowing that every effort, every tear, and every smile makes a difference.

BEING a foster carer is one of the most challenging yet rewarding roles imaginable. It saddens me deeply to see so many carers in Australia walking away. I understand why they leave—the system is flawed, and the work is gruelling. But if we all give up, nothing will ever change.

I get so discouraged hearing comments from carers saying, "It will never change, so why bother?" Maybe they're right. Maybe the system will always be imperfect. But that doesn't mean the kids don't need us. They do. And unless some of us stay in the game, the system's failures will continue to define the future for too many children.

A Better Way Forward

Foster care is not just a system—it's a network of people doing their best to support vulnerable children, often within a framework that feels deeply flawed. Caseworkers, agencies, carers, and policymakers all play a role in shaping the experiences of these children. But too often, their efforts are hindered by bureaucracy, inefficiency, and a lack of genuine collaboration.

Over the years, I've seen the best and worst of the system. I've witnessed dedicated caseworkers burn out; their passion smothered under mountains of paperwork. I've met carers who poured their hearts into children, only to walk away because they felt unsupported and undervalued. And worst of all, I've seen children—real, living, breathing kids—caught in the crossfire of poor decisions, outdated policies, and a system more focused on protocols than people.

Despite these challenges, I still believe in foster care. I believe in the ability of carers, agencies, and communities to create something better. But to do that, we have to acknowledge what's broken and have the courage to demand change.

THE CHALLENGES in foster care don't fall on one person or group. Caseworkers, agencies, carers, and the government all play a role, often interwoven with each other's successes and failures. Caseworkers frequently enter the field with the best intentions, driven by a desire to protect and support vulnerable children. However, many burn out under the crushing weight of overwhelming caseloads, endless paperwork, and rigid policies that leave little room for creative problem-solving. Statistics show that turnover rates in child protection are alarmingly high, with caseworkers leaving within a few years of starting because of stress and lack of support. Those who stay often lose the passion and energy that brought them to the job in the first place, leaving an already strained system even weaker.

Agencies, though often well-meaning, are deeply bound by the political and funding landscape. Budgets frequently dictate decisions, and protocols aimed at managing risk can sometimes hinder the ability to respond flexibly to individual cases. Carers, too, feel the strain. Many enter fostering with open hearts, but frustration builds as they navigate a system that seems more focused on bureaucracy than on the needs of the children they care for. Without adequate training, resources, or emotional support, many carers give up altogether, further exacerbating the crisis.

Ultimately, we are all responsible. Children are the most vulnerable in our society, and it is our collective duty to ensure their well-being is prioritised. Foster care and adoption in Australia need systemic change. Policies must be overhauled to prioritise the developmental needs of children, reducing delays in permanency decisions and addressing the complex barriers to guardianship and adoption. The government must treat child welfare as a national priority, allocating sufficient resources to train and retain caseworkers and reduce their caseloads. Agencies need to advocate fiercely for the children in their care, pushing against restrictive policies that leave them powerless. Carers must be equipped—not just with practical training and resources but also with emotional and therapeutic support to handle the challenges of fostering.

We cannot afford to allow these problems to continue unchecked. Every day of uncertainty in a child's life is a day of lost stability, lost growth, and lost opportunity. Whether it's by fostering, advocating for policy change, or supporting carers and caseworkers, we all have a role to play. The question isn't just *who's responsible*—it's how each of us can step up to make a difference.

I dream of a foster care system that truly prioritises children—a system built on compassion, respect, and collaboration. Maybe I'll see it in my lifetime; maybe I won't. But I believe change is possible.

For those of you who have given up on the system, I understand. It's exhausting. The victories often feel overshadowed by the constant frustrations, the endless red tape, and the heartbreaking setbacks. But I haven't given up. I believe in the power of community, in the strength of carers, and in the possibility of creating a better future for these children—if we work together.

I DREAM of carers supported with interconnected networks, with the resources and supports they need to do the role well. For the kids to receive the care they deserve. I dream of foster carers united in supportive communities. Imagine neighbourhoods built with foster families in mind: a place where carers and children feel less isolated and where they can share resources, advice, and emotional support. We could build networks of connections where people understand the unique joys and challenges of fostering and where children in care can find stability, belonging, and a sense of normalcy.

Alongside this book, I'm working hard on other projects to see real change come. I'm no longer waiting for someone else to create change; my team and I are doing it now. There is an urgent need for stronger support, community, and well-being resources for foster carers across Australia. My hope is that as we collaborate

—carers, agencies, and community members—we will see a meaningful shift in the foster care system.

ONE SIGNIFICANT BARRIER foster carers face is finances. With the rising cost of living, many households need two incomes to stay afloat. Foster care is no different, yet many of these children need a stay-at-home parent due to the trauma they carry. Even in cases labelled "normal," these kids need someone who can stay home when they're sick, take them to endless therapy appointments, coordinate family time, meet with caseworkers, and manage home visits.

This expectation can be overwhelming. One carer shared with me, "I just always dropped something when I tried to do both work and foster care." If carers had the financial freedom to focus entirely on the children in their care, it would transform their ability to parent effectively. No one should have to fight to get school fees paid or wonder if they can afford groceries because they're fostering.

Let's be clear: needing financial support doesn't mean carers are in it for the money. Everyone works to pay their bills—why should foster carers be any different? The real issue is whether carers are given the resources they need to meet the children's needs.

THE LACK of emotional support for carers is another glaring issue. Foster carers often do the hardest work imaginable, but are treated as though their contributions don't matter. They endure sleepless nights, tantrums, birth family issues and appointments, yet the respect they receive from agencies and society often falls short. Many carers feel abandoned by agencies and the system.

Carers need more than acknowledgment—they need genuine support. If carers were treated with the same respect as employees or colleagues, the retention rates would improve, and so would the overall quality of care for the children.

Carers are the backbone of the system, and the children need them. Agencies don't heal kids—carers do. Carers are the ones up at night, comforting tears, managing behaviours, and showing unconditional love. They're the ones holding these children together through the chaos.

I've heard many carers say they'd never recommend fostering because it's so hard. I've had those same thoughts. But it always comes back to the kids. Despite the brokenness of the system, these children deserve safe, loving homes. They deserve carers willing to wade through the hard moments to give them a shot at healing.

As a carer, it's easy to wonder if your efforts matter. I've held children in my arms, poured love into them, and questioned whether my hugs and care will have a lasting impact. Will it all be erased when they leave? It's a haunting question, but I believe the answer is yes—we are making a difference, even if it's only for a short time. Every moment of love, every bit of stability, plants seeds of healing.

EVERYONE in this system has opinions, and emotions often run high. Australia's history with the Stolen Generations adds a complex layer to every conversation about child welfare. While those atrocities must never be forgotten, we must also find a new way forward. Every child, regardless of their background, deserves a loving, stable home where they can thrive.

Tension often arises between those prioritising restoration with birth relatives and those advocating for alternative permanent solutions, such as permanent care, guardianship or adoption. Restoration is undoubtedly a worthy goal—it seeks to mend fractured families and honour cultural connections—but it cannot come at the expense of a child's safety, stability, or well-being. After two years in care, policy requires that a final decision be made whether restoration to the birth family will occur or not. Two years is far too long for a toddler to live in limbo, waiting for a decision about their future. And yet, even after two years, agencies sometimes continue to push for restoration, leaving children trapped in an endless cycle of uncertainty. If we as adults struggle with the uncertainty of placements—how much harder must it be for a child?

The government's policies need to reflect the urgency of a child's developmental needs—especially during those critical early years when the foundations of emotional regulation, trust, and identity are formed. Disruptions in attachment during this stage can have lifelong implications, affecting a child's ability to form healthy relationships, manage emotions, and feel secure in the world.

Yet guardianship and adoption processes are often stalled because birth parents refuse consent, even after being deemed unfit. At what point do we shift the focus from parental rights to the child's right to stability? After two years—or even sooner—the priority must become the child's long-term well-being, not the preservation of a connection that continues to delay permanency and healing.

If someone expresses an interest in adoption from the outset, agencies often roll their eyes or treat it as a misguided ambition. Within Australia, options for direct adoption are limited. It's possible, but it remains a long and gruelling process. According to the Australian Institute of Health and Welfare (AIHW), only 207 adoptions were finalised in 2023–2024, representing a significant decline from previous years. With there being over 45,000 children in foster care, many of whom need long-term placements, permanency planning must be made a priority. The low number of adoptions isn't due to a shortage of children needing forever homes but is more a reflection of the complex process and political barriers that stand in the way. Thousands of children remain in limbo, longing for the love, security and permanence they deserve.

IF WE ARE serious about creating a better system for children and carers, some basic things need to change:

- **Respect for Carers:** Carers are the backbone of the foster care system, yet they are often treated as secondary to agency staff. Carers must be treated as valuable partners, with their input sought and respected in decisions about the children in their care.
- **Adequate Resources:** Children in foster care deserve the best chance at a happy, healthy life, and this means meeting their needs. Financial and practical support must be provided promptly and adequately to ensure children have everything they need to thrive.
- **Emotional Support for Carers:** The emotional toll of fostering is immense. Carers need access to counselling, peer support groups, and other mental health resources to sustain them through the highs and lows of fostering.
- **Community Support:** Carers and children alike benefit when communities rally around them. Schools, churches, local businesses, and neighbours all have roles to play in creating a network of care and understanding for foster families.
- **Timelines for Adoption and Guardianship:** The drawn-out timelines for adoption and guardianship need to be drastically improved. Every delay prolongs uncertainty for children and families, making it harder for everyone involved to build stable lives.
- **Timely Support for Children:** Children in care often wait far too long for psychological services, occupational therapy, assessments, and specialist care. Early and consistent intervention can change the trajectory of a child's life.

- **More Caseworkers with Smaller Caseloads:** Overworked caseworkers cannot effectively meet the needs of children and carers. We need more caseworkers with smaller caseloads to ensure that every child and carer receives the attention and support they deserve.
- **Collaboration Between Agencies:** Agencies must stop operating in silos and start working together. A more unified approach can prevent children from falling through the cracks and ensure resources are distributed more effectively.

HOPE. A word in which I continue to find meaning. Something that I've realised I can never let go of. I hold on to the hope that these changes are possible. It won't happen overnight, and it won't be easy, but I believe in the power of persistence. If carers, agencies, caseworkers, and communities come together with a shared vision, we can create a system that prioritises the well-being of every child in care.

At times, I have judged harshly. I've been critical of caseworkers, frustrated with birth parents, even other carers. I questioned the decisions and assumed I knew better. And for that, I'm sorry. Foster care is hard. We're all doing the best we can with the tools we have—and sometimes, we don't have the right ones yet. Instead of judging each other for how we're coping (or not coping), maybe we could try something else. Maybe we offer a hand. A listening ear. A little grace. We all want what's best for the children. Let's start there.

The road ahead may be long, but the destination—a system built on respect, compassion, and genuine care—is worth striving for. Because every child deserves a chance to feel safe, loved, and supported. And every carer deserves to feel valued in the role they play in making that happen.

When I first started, I thought everyone should foster. Then, I saw how hard it was and felt I couldn't recommend it to anyone. But now, I see it differently. No, it's not for everyone, but more people could do it than those who currently are.

If you're considering fostering, my advice is this: Do it. It will be one of the hardest things you'll ever do, but it's worth it. If you need a break, take one. But don't give up. The kids need you.

The foster care system is far from perfect, but the children need us. They need people willing to fight for them, to advocate for change, and to love them through their struggles. Advocacy and education are key to creating a better future. The system may be broken, but it's not beyond repair. Every effort matters. Every child deserves a chance.

Appendix

This appendix provides a general overview of the application and assessment process for becoming a foster carer in Australia. While not exhaustive or specific to every state or agency, it provides practical tips and insights to help prospective carers understand what to expect and how to prepare.

While this section is based on my experience as a carer and a foster care agency worker, every Australian state and territory operates slightly differently in how they assess, approve and support foster carers. Be sure to check the requirements specific to your region through your local department or a foster care support organisation.

Choosing the Right Agency

This is a big decision. And can be a challenging one. It's challenging because everyone has a different experience with each agency. One person will have a terrible experience with an agency, and the next has nothing but good things to say about it. It really is an individual choice and sometimes a matter of luck. I've worked for an agency that had multiple offices. One office did an amazing job caring for their carers, while the office in a different region had many disgruntled carers. I've been with agencies where we were treated poorly, but the carer beside me had a wonderful experience. No two stories are the same. Ask around the local carers in your area. Ask them about their experience, but also try to gauge, if you can, if they are so consumed with frustration with the system that their opinion is skewed by this anger. Would they recommend fostering at all?

Remember, you can always change agencies. We stayed with an agency for longer than we should have, hoping things would improve. In hindsight, we should have transferred to another agency sooner. Once we switched, we had other challenges, but they were ones we could manage—ones others might find harder than we did. Every agency has its strengths and weaknesses; the key is finding the one that fits you best.

Another thing to consider is the political landscape at the time. Different state governments periodically complete inquiries into their child safety or out-of-home care systems. It's worth keeping informed about the reviews and reforms occurring in your state or territory. Each state has different legislation, so it's important to do your research. Each state and territory has a different approach to funding, agency contracts and policy frameworks. This means the experience of foster care can vary significantly depending on where you live—even between neighbouring regions.

The Assessment Process

Each agency does things a little differently, but here is an overview of what the process looks like to become a foster carer:

Screening Phone Call

>At this stage, you'll speak with a worker on the phone who will assess your suitability to become a foster carer. They will inquire about various aspects of your life,

including your job, financial stability, motivations for fostering, and knowledge of foster care. Sensitive questions may also arise, such as whether you've experienced infertility, your physical and mental health, and relationship status, as part of understanding your background, reasons for applying, to ensure that unsuitable applicants are screened out.

Information Exchange

This is the stage where a worker or two will come to your home, give you the application paperwork, and conduct probity checks. They'll have another conversation with you about foster care, what to expect, what type of care you want to provide, and your motivations.

Application and Probity Checks Documents:

- Application Form
- Working with Children Check (or equivalent)
- Criminal History Checks
- Health Checks—filled out by your doctor
- Home Safety Check

Training

Training requirements vary slightly across states and agencies, but typically include a short foundational course over 2 days. You'll learn about trauma, how to care for traumatised children, what's required of you as a carer, working with the birth family, and working with the agency. This is entry-level training in foster care. For many, if not most, further training should be sought.

Assessment

The assessor or agency will follow a structured assessment, which typically includes a 5-session interviewing process, each lasting around two hours. You will go through your ability to provide care and safety, your family and trauma history, your relationships, your support network, your willingness to support children's birth family, and cultural connections. Timelines for assessment can vary significantly. Some can take only a few months, while others can take 12 months or more. This can all depend on your availability for meetings, your assessor's workload, how quickly paperwork and checks are completed and if any concerns or complexities arise during the assessment.

Panel

Once your assessment meetings and documents are complete, your full application and assessment report will be presented to a panel. A panel is a group of managers who review your application and assessment to determine whether you are suitable for approval as a carer.

Each panels operate a little differently. Some take a balanced, trauma-informed approach, while others may focus heavily on minor details, making the process feel overly critical at times. It helps to remember their job is due diligence. The panel's primary responsibility is to ensure the safety and well-being of a child—which is vital. They may request additional documents to assess your suitability, ask you to speak with a professional, or require more evidence of specific capabilities or stability.
From my experience—as both a foster parent and an agency worker—the process can sometimes feel skewed toward identifying weaknesses rather than noticing strengths or the support that could help the potential carer thrive. As an applicant, this can be overwhelming

and, at times, feel unfair. But try to remember: this is the final step before approval. Hold onto that.

Approval

If the panel agrees that you should be a carer, then you will get approval. You'll be approved for a certain age range and number of kids. You'll receive an official letter of authorisation and be registered on your state's child protection carer register.

You're Approved—Now What?

It's a common experience for carers to get approved and then wait weeks or even months without a placement. This can be baffling, especially when there's a clear outcry for more carers. Why the delay after approval? There are several reasons for this.

Sometimes, the issue lies with the agency. They might not have enough caseworkers to manage additional children or the capacity to take on new placements. Agencies also screen children carefully to ensure the right match. Even in emergencies, they may decline to place a child with you if they don't think it will be a suitable fit. This process is aimed at protecting both carers and children, reducing the risk of placement breakdowns.

For example, if you're a new carer with no prior experience raising or caring for traumatised children, the agency may be cautious about placing a child with unknown or complex needs in your care. They aim to set everyone up for success, which can mean taking time to find the right match.

Another factor is the age group you're open to fostering. If you're hoping for a single child under five for a long-term placement, the wait can be longer. Younger children are often the focus of restoration efforts, as the system prioritises keeping them with their birth families whenever possible.

That said, placements can happen quickly, too. Sometimes, you'll get a call within days of approval—perhaps for respite care or a crisis placement that could even turn into a long-term arrangement.

Tips for New & Aspiring Foster Carers

Things Happen Slowly – it's important to understand that the foster care system often operates at a different pace. Whether it's a school change, financial reimbursement, court outcomes, placement decision, or family time arrangements, things can take much longer than expected. Prepare yourself to wait and try to be as patient as you can. To help with this, ask your caseworker for clear next steps and regular updates in writing.

It's Usually not Personal – Most people in the system—assessors, caseworkers, agency staff—aren't out to attack you. They're doing their jobs within the limits of policy, paperwork, and accountability. Sometimes it may feel like they're being overly cautious or critical, but often, it's about protecting themselves and the agency if something goes wrong—not about judging your worth. It's human nature. Try not to take it to heart.

People will Hurt You—but it's Rarely About You – This journey will involve pain. Children might push you away. Agencies might disappoint you. Friends or family might not understand. It's easy to feel hurt and take things personally—but often, it's not about you. It's about their own fears, trauma, or limitations. That doesn't mean the pain isn't real—but it does mean you can practice letting go of what doesn't belong to you. Keep trying. It gets easier over time.

Find Other Carers – it's a hard journey, and it should not be taken alone. Find other carers to reach out to, but also be careful who you listen to. Some carers are very scared of the system and their experience. Remember, their experience might not be yours. Find a variety of carers if possible—those who understand the uniqueness of the journey and who you can reach out to when things get tough.

Keep Learning – Books, podcasts, and other carers' stories can offer valuable insight into the world of foster care. While nothing fully prepares you for the lived experience, learning from others can help you feel more equipped and less alone. Stories can spark understanding, shift your mindset, and remind you that what you're feeling is normal. Keep seeking out knowledge—it adds up, and it makes a difference.

Normalise Hard Days – Some days will feel overwhelming. You might wonder, *Why am I struggling so much? Why does everything feel so hard?* It's because it *is* hard. Parenting is hard. Fostering is hard. Navigating caseworkers, trauma, family time, uncertainty, and goodbyes—it's all heavy, emotional work. Struggling doesn't mean you're doing it wrong. It means you're human. Give yourself permission to feel it, and reach out when you need support. Hard days are part of the journey—not a sign you shouldn't be on it.

Recommended Reading and Viewing

I've compiled a list of a few resources that I've found helpful on our journey. I've felt isolated navigating foster care, but in those moments when I heard other stories and got relevant information, it was so helpful. Each one of these resources provided me with a greater understanding of foster care and adoption. Some of them are stories of other people's journeys, while others offer more practical advice.

- *The Post Adoption Blues* by Karen J. Foli and John R. Thompson
- *Confessions of an Adoptive Parent* by Mike Berry
- *The Foster Care Survival Guide* by Dr. John DeGarmo
- *Fostering* by Carmen Maria Navarro
- *Murder, Motherhood and Miraculous Grace* by Debra Moerke
- *Trying* (Apple TV): A heartfelt portrayal of foster care adoption
- *A-Z of Parenting* by Sarah Naish
- Books by Maggie Hartley
- Books by Louise Allen

Foster care is an endeavour filled with uncertainties and obstacles, but it is also one of profound significance. The steps to becoming a carer are not simple, and the road is rarely smooth, but the difference you can make in a child's life is immeasurable. Every act of kindness, stability, and love you provide helps shape their journey, even if only for a short time. While the system may be slow and imperfect, your role as a foster carer can bring moments of healing and hope to children who desperately need it. If you're considering this path, it will be one of the hardest things you'll ever do, but it's also one of the most meaningful. Know that you are not alone—resources, support, and community are there to help you succeed. Together, we can create brighter futures for these children, one placement at a time.

www.ingramcontent.com/pod-product-compliance
Lightning Source LLC
Chambersburg PA
CBHW020536080526
44583CB00013B/883